G. K. Chesterton, Theologian

Aidan Nichols, O.P.

G. K. Chesterton,
Theologian

Second
Spring
from
SOPHIA INSTITUTE PRESS®

Manchester, New Hampshire

Sophia Institute Press®
Box 5284, Manchester, NH 03108
1-800-888-9344
www.sophiainstitute.com

Library of Congress Cataloging-in-Publication Data

Nichols, Aidan.
    G.K. Chesterton, theologian / Aidan Nichols.
       p. cm.
    Includes bibliographical references.
    ISBN 978-1-933184-50-0 (pbk. : alk. paper) 1. Chesterton,
      G. K. (Gilbert Keith), 1874-1936 — Criticism and interpretation. 2. Chesterton, G. K. (Gilbert Keith), 1874-1936
      — Religion. 3. Theology in literature. I. Title.
    PR4453.C4Z735 2009
    823'.912 — dc22

                                  2009005822

For John Osman

Contents

Preface

This study has a straightforward form. The book falls, in effect, into two halves. The first opens by offering an overview of Chesterton's life, an overview that already identifies some salient intellectual themes. Chapter 2, on the Edwardian writers who were his earliest controversial opponents, chiefly explores materials found in his first major work, *Heretics*. Chapter 3 centres on *Orthodoxy*, which Chesterton intended to be read with *Heretics* in one's other hand, though it also ranges more widely in detailing Chesterton's "discovery of metaphysical realism," his version of Catholic Christianity's *philosophia perennis*. Chapter 4 investigates the most distinctive of Chesterton's imaginative and argumentative strategies, the paradox.

Then in the second half of this enquiry, I consider five theological themes: Chesterton's argument for the existence of God, his theological anthropology, his Christology, his moral theology, and his ecclesiology — or, more widely, his overall sense of the Catholic Church and her faith.

Alison Milbank's study of Chesterton and Tolkien as theologians reached me too late for me to profit from it in the present study (as did also William Oddie's marvellously detailed study of

Chesterton's early years). I am delighted to see, however, that she looks in this direction for light. I hope that, in the wake of her more ambitious work, this modest book will help to encourage theological interest in Chesterton, and indeed, the interest of Chestertonians in theology.

Aidan Nichols, O.P.
Blackfriars, Cambridge
Ash Wednesday, 2008

Introduction

It is not customary to consider G. K. Chesterton a theologian, although his sympathy with theologians is unmistakable. In *Christendom in Dublin* he registered his annoyance with the "tired and tiresome voice of the general scepticism" which "talks with eternal reiteration about the quarrels of theologians."

> One would suppose that nobody had ever quarrelled except theologians; or that theologians had never done anything else. But if there be one thing morally certain, it is that the world will quarrel much more without theology than it ever did with theology.[1]

Chesterton considered this self-evident, since "people left without any common theory, or attempt at a theory, will be able to quarrel about absolutely anything whatever; including all the things on which men have hitherto agreed."[2] Modern thinkers can and do take up ultimate positions which all past theologians would have termed "anarchical and abnormal." It is hard to dislodge these

---

[1] *Christendom in Dublin* (London, 1932), 41-42.

[2] Ibid., 42.

positions precisely because they *are* ultimate: "They are out of sight and hearing, for the purpose of anything so sociable as a quarrel. Men do not agree enough to disagree."[3] How, for example, can one reason with someone who denies the validity of reason? Or what is the point of proving unjust someone who does not believe in justice? "It is idle to offer ocular demonstration to the really consistent sceptic, who cannot believe his eyes."[4]

> Once remove the old arena of theological quarrels, and you will throw open the whole world to the most horrible, the most hopeless, the most endless, the most truly interminable quarrels; the untheological quarrels.[5]

So winning a statement should not go without its theological reward.

Chesterton's Theological Help

That is one reason for writing this book. Moreover, Chesterton has not only praised theologians; he has helped them. In the face of an agnosticism that has set its face against Christianity, he is attractive, indeed persuasive. As he put it with characteristic winningness in his study of William Blake:

> You cannot take the region called the unknown and calmly say that though you know nothing about it, you know that all its gates are locked. That was the whole fallacy of Herbert Spencer and Huxley when they talked about the unknowable instead of about the unknown. An agnostic like Huxley must concede the possibility of a gnostic like Blake.

---

[3] *Christendom in Dublin*, 43.

[4] Ibid.

[5] Ibid.

We do not know enough about the unknown to know that it is unknowable.[6]

And since Chesterton was never afraid of risk-taking with his readership, he would go further:

When Blake lived at Felpham angels appear to have been as native to the Sussex trees as birds. His patriarchs walked on the Sussex Downs as easily as if they were in the desert.

Should we simply say, then, asks Chesterton, that Blake was mad? He replies: "Surely we cannot take an open question like the supernatural and shut it with a bang, turning the key of the madhouse on all the mystics of history."[7]

In "The Curse of the Golden Cross," Father Brown is made to declare, "I can believe the impossible, but not the improbable." The Byronic young American Paul T. Tarrant asks, "That's what you call a paradox, isn't it?"

"It's what I call common sense, properly understood," replied Father Brown. "It really is more natural to believe a preternatural story, that deals with things we don't understand, than a natural story that contradicts things we do understand. Tell me that the great Mr Gladstone, in his last hours, was haunted by the ghost of Parnell, and I will be agnostic about it. But tell me that Mr Gladstone, when first presented to Queen Victoria, wore his hat in her drawing-room and slapped her on the back and offered her a cigar, and I am not agnostic at all. That is not impossible, it's only incredible."[8]

---

[6] *William Blake* (London, 1910), 74.

[7] Ibid., 73.

[8] *The Complete Father Brown Stories* (London, 1992, 2006), 431.

G. K. Chesterton, Theologian

Chesterton may not have considered himself a theologian. But he knew that theology was thought applied to religion, and as Stratford Caldecott remarks, "Very few have applied thought to religion as effectively as he."[9]

Chesterton and the English
Contribution to Catholicity

Another reason, and a more autobiographical one, for writing this book, is bound up with my own latest excuse for returning to Chesterton. In a recent book, I selected him as one of half a dozen or so "sages" or "critics of the culture" who might help to re-launch the mission of a Christian intelligentsia in contemporary English society. In *The Realm: An Unfashionable Essay on the Conversion of England*, I confessed my admiration for Chesterton's approach to apologetics: how Christianity satisfies at one and the same time our deep conviction that we are at home in the world — and yet do not really belong to it.[10] I suggested that *Orthodoxy* remains for the English the best introduction to Gospel religion.[11]

Chesterton also has much to offer the wider cause of reconstructing English identity, since his prescription in the 1920s is as pertinent now as it was then: "What is wanted for the cause of England today is an Englishman with enough imagination to love his country from the outside as well as the inside."[12] Chesterton

---

[9] S. Caldecott, "Was Chesterton a Theologian?" *The Chesterton Review* XXIV.4 (1998): 465.

[10] A. Nichols, O.P., *The Realm: An Unfashionable Essay on the Conversion of England* (Oxford, 2008), 110-118.

[11] Orthodoxy, of course, abounds in paradoxes, and Chesterton himself has left an essay, reprinted in the posthumous collection *The Glass Walking-stick*, where he roundly declares that "the English people have a peculiar appetite for paradox."

[12] *What I saw in America* (London, 1922), 284.

disliked homogenisation. "Nations can love each other as men and women love each other, not because they are alike but because they are different."[13] He wanted a cultural-theological vindication of "the spirit of England": "to make England attractive as a nationality, and even as a small nationality."[14] I am inclined to trust his judgements owing to his sympathy with culture both low and high, and to the assurance and congeniality with which he moved among the classics of the English literary canon. Let us add, too, in the latter connection, his generosity of spirit, as in this encomium on Thomas Hardy:

> People talk of the pessimism of Hardy as ruthless, and in its artistic method it was ruthless, often at the expense of reason and probability. But if he changed spiritually, it was always towards feeling less of the ruthlessness and more of the ruth. I should be very much surprised to learn that Hardy, especially in later life, was really a pessimist at all. His theory, as a theory, is not very clear or complete; but I am sure he did not become more clear or more complete, in the sense of more convinced of a dogma of despair.[15]

If England can make any specific contribution to catholicity, it is probably along the lines of the literary expression of humaneness. Such humaneness of spirit has its foundation in the enduring good sense of a post-lapsarian humanity that, in the formulations of Trent over against the Reformers, may be wounded, but is not for that reason a "dead duck." There is something living here on which grace can build. Chesterton praised the "richness and

---

[13] Ibid., 285.

[14] Ibid.

[15] *Come to Think of It* (London, 1930), 129.

humanity of the unconscious tradition" of the age into which he was born, despite the "cheapness and narrowness of its conscious formulae."[16] He saw in that dull monarch George V, who occupied the throne for the last quarter-century of Chesterton's adult life, someone who represented the "protection of the patient and unrecorded virtues of mankind."[17] Chesterton did not rule out the possibility "in the incalculable time before us" that:

> there may return to the mystical institution of the Crown something of that immemorial legend which linked it with religion, and made one baron, alone of all the barony, mysteriously responsible to God for the people.[18]

In England today, among people of sensibility, the chief substitutes for religion are "spirituality" and aestheticism. Chesterton had long since seen through them. He isolated the religiose but fundamentally agnostic panacea that now goes by the convenient name, at once vague and benign, of "spirituality," and which Matthew Arnold called "culture": "the disinterested play of the mind through the sifting of the best books and authors."[19] To preserve a Church as a "vessel to contain the spiritual ideas of the age, whatever those ideas may be,"[20] could be considered the work of the culture-vultures "trying to establish and endow Agnosticism." But, declares Chesterton:

> [I]t is fairer and truer to say that unconsciously [Arnold] was trying to restore Paganism: for this State Ritualism without

[16] *The Victorian Age in Literature* (London, 1911), 31.
[17] *Come to Think of It*, 242.
[18] Ibid.
[19] *The Victorian Age in Literature*, 73.
[20] Ibid., 76.

theology, and without much belief, actually was the practice of the ancient world.[21]

Regarding aestheticism, Chesterton also identified — in John Ruskin — the habit of mind that decides to "accept Catholic art but not Catholic ethics."[22] The phenomenally well-attended National Gallery exhibition *Seeing Salvation* did not, one supposes, find an ecclesial correlative in a greatly increased rate of conversion to the Catholic Church, even though that Church was the inspiration of the vast majority of the artworks involved. Again, as Chesterton remarks:

> In the matter of religion (which was the key of this age as of every other) [Ruskin] did not, like Carlyle, set up the romance of the great Puritans as a rival to the romance of the Catholic Church. Rather, he set up and worshipped all the arts and trophies of the Catholic Church as a rival to the Church itself.[23]

To link Chesterton so strongly to an analysis of the soul of England may not be the best way to commend this book to non-English readers. Yet Chesterton is a quintessentially English author, and, moreover, the catholicity of the Church is incomplete until all the nations have made their contribution to it. In that sense, it is Chesterton's very Englishness that makes him of greatest interest to Catholics in America and elsewhere. And while we are still thinking of Chesterton from the viewpoint of the England — or the wider Christian world — of the early twenty-first century, I do not suppose many people will query the "prophetic"

[21] *The Victorian Age in Literature*, 77.

[22] Ibid., 69.

[23] Ibid., 62-63.

character of Chesterton's comment — made in 1911! — to the effect that Mohammed "created a very big thing, which we have still to deal with."[24]

No doubt we shall contend with this "very big thing" — if disproportionate fears of terrorism do not prevent us — in a gentlemanly and sensible fashion. As Chesterton put it in his *Autobiography*, "sleepy sanity" is a typical English trait.[25] Sometimes, however, we need a wake-up call — of the kind given by the Victorian giants on whom he wrote so well: Ruskin, Carlyle, Morris, Newman, and the rest. The remainder of this book seeks to show that "Chesterton's theology" is just that.

[24] *The Victorian Age in Literature*, 44.
[25] *Autobiography* (London, 1936), 35-36.

G. K. Chesterton, Theologian

Chapter 1

An Overview of Chesterton's Life

G. K. Chesterton was born in 1874, in west central London, between Holland Park and Kensington Palace Gardens, the elder son
of an estate agent whose family had long been established in that
business. Like many middle-class people, adequately supplied with
servants, and funded by family firms that more or less ran themselves, his father and mother had a good deal of leisure time which
they devoted to artistic or quasi-artistic pastimes, including water-
colour painting, toy theatres, photography, collecting mediaeval
illuminations and stained glass, and the study and memorisation of
English literature.[26] They were Liberals with a capital L in politics
and a small l in religion, occasionally attending a Unitarian chapel
in the vicinity. Chesterton's younger brother Cecil would sum up
their creed as "the Fatherhood of God, the Brotherhood of Man,
the non-eternity of evil, the final salvation of souls": all amounting

[26] Toy theatres figured large in Chesterton's childhood: it is instructive that in his study of Stevenson he ascribes to the Scots novelist's own childhood love for them the origin of the "special style
or spirit" of his work in its clarity of form and characterisation.
"In that little pasteboard play, there might be something of the
pantomime, but there was nothing of the dissolving view," *Robert
Louis Stevenson* (London, 1927), 50.

to what he termed "a vague but noble theo-philanthropy."[27] At least it was a creed of a sort. The Chestertons' household may have coincided with, but did not exemplify, what Chesterton called "the precise moment when a middle-class man still had children and servants to control but no longer had creeds or guilds or kings or priests to control him"; such a man was thus "an anarchist to those above him, but still an authoritarian to those below."[28]

Through no fault of his educators, Chesterton's schooling was erratic. But as an adult he believed strongly in the prolongation of childhood, and he never regretted that he had been a backward child. He attended St Paul's School at a time when it enjoyed un-doubted academic excellence, yet he was noted for inattention, slovenliness of personal appearance, and incompetence at sport, although because he was taller than most other boys as well as — at this juncture — still slim, he escaped bullying. The ongoing in-formal education he received from his father, who took him to mu-seums and galleries, and explored with him the literary classics, counted for more than his lessons. Where Chesterton came alive at school was as chairman of the St Paul's Junior Debating Club and contributor to its short-lived but professionally produced magazine, *The Debater*, in whose pages his originality of thought and expression, and gifts of versification — all typified by remark-able energy and exuberance — became apparent for the first time. The mediocrity of his form reports stood in sharp contrast to the judgement given his mother by the High Master of the school in 1894: "Six foot of genius. Cherish him, Mrs Chesterton, cherish him."[29]

---

[27] Cited in M. Ffinch, *G. K. Chesterton* (London, 1986), 13.

[28] *Autobiography*, 21.

[29] Cited in M. Ward, *Gilbert Keith Chesterton* (London, 1945), 42.

Chesterton's gift for friendship, which would later metamorphose into the capacity to capture the goodwill of a far wider range of people than is the lot of most of us, had also emerged by this time, the best-known of his close companions being Edmund Clerihew Bentley, inventor of the minor genre known by his middle name. "The people of Spain think Cervantes/ Equal to half-a-dozen Dantes,/ An opinion resented most bitterly/ By the people of Italy." Unlike his friends, however, Chesterton did not go up to Oxford or Cambridge. He had shown minimal academic as distinct from intellectual ability. Instead, following his own inclination and with parental encouragement, he attended drawing classes and subsequently the Slade School of Fine Art, at that period a department of University College, London, where Chesterton also took some non-examined courses in English and French and, for a short while, Latin. After a year, he was asked to leave, since his teachers considered they had failed to teach him anything beyond the skills of decorative and grotesque drawing skills he already possessed.

Crisis and Reaction

Chesterton's experience of the Slade is nonetheless important for his biography and also for the history of his opinions. Influenced by some of its students and, one can speculate, depressed by the loss of his buddies who were either still enrolled at school or, in due course, went up to the historic universities, he began to feel, by his own account (see his "notebooks"[30] and *Autobiography*, for instance), a distinct attraction toward evil.[31] He gravitated towards

---

[30] A miscellaneous collection of documents now in the G. K. Chesterton Archives in the Manuscripts Department of the British Library.

[31] See W. Oddie, "Chesterton at the *Fin de siècle*: Orthodoxy and the Perception of Evil," *The Chesterton Review* XXV.3 (1999), 329-343.

nihilism as a general philosophy of life and began to dabble in occultist spiritualism. Spiritualism was becoming fashionable, especially among the metropolitan elite, but Chesterton's taste of it, and conversations with students whom he took, at any rate, to be diabolists, was salutary.[32] His agnosticism remained, but it acquired a pro-Christian colouration. For instance, at some point in this period he jotted down about Christmas Day, "Good news: but if you ask me what it is, I know not;/ It is a track of feet in the snow, It is a lantern showing a path, It is a door set open."[33]

At the Slade Chesterton also acquired an extremely hostile attitude to the painterly mode called Impressionism, a hostility that not only later defined much of his attitude to art at large but was formative for the development of his realism in metaphysics. Consider his 1907 novel, *The Man Who Was Thursday*. As Gabriel Syme, fleeing from the agents of Sunday, dives into a patch of woodland, the play of light and shade on the leaves causes him to muse:

> Was not everything, after all, like this bewildering woodland, this dance of dark and light? Everything only a glimpse, the glimpse always unforeseen, and always forgotten. For Gabriel Syme had found in the heart of that sun-splashed wood what many modern painters had found there. He had found the thing the modern people called Impressionism, which is another name for that final scepticism which can find no floor to the universe.[34]

---

[32] In his 1913 play *Magic* he "plainly stated that calling up powers, thrones, and dominations was an ancient and perilous sin," A. S. Dale, *The Outline of Sanity: A Life of G. K. Chesterton* (Grand Rapids, Michigan, 1982), 35.

[33] Cited in M. Ward, *Gilbert Keith Chesterton*, 62.

[34] *The Man Who Was Thursday* (London, 1907, 1944), 131. For an analysis of Chesterton's attitude to Impressionism, see J. D.

The identification of Impressionism as a symptom of cultural and, especially, epistemological decadence also finds expression in, for example, his 1910 study of William Blake. Seeking to express how for Blake lucidity and decisiveness of outline were the chief desiderata in draftsmanship, Chesterton risks the anachronism of writing that "the thing he hated most in art was the thing which we now call Impressionism — the substitution of atmosphere for shape, the sacrifice of form to tint, the cloudland of the mere colourist." Incidentally, that same work ascribes the presence of occasional bizarre phrases, sometimes obsessively repeated, in Blake's poetry to his commerce with spirits — not all of which were necessarily benign. Chesterton's Slade experience provides the likely context for such assessments as the following:

> It was exactly because [Blake] was unnaturally exposed to a hail of forces that were more than natural that some breaches were made in his mental continuity, some damage was done to his mind.[35]

More widely, Chesterton's dip into the waters of *fin-de-siècle* aestheticism gave him an aversion to any variant on "art for art's sake," an aesthetic, he thought, that licensed a willful departure from the real — both in the sense of showing a lack of respect for given natural forms and in the sense of departure from moral norms themselves warranted by humanity's good sense. That is a motif of his first published work, *Greybeards at Play*, a collection of comic verse subsidised by his father. W. H. Auden thought it some of the best of its kind in English.

Coates, *Chesterton and the Edwardian Cultural Crisis* (Hull, 1984), 191-209.

[35] *William Blake*, 94.

G. K. Chesterton, Theologian

I had a rather funny dream,
Intense, that is, and mystic;
I dreamed that, with one leap and yell,
The world became artistic.
The Shopmen, when their souls were still,
Declined to open shops —
And cooks recorded frames of mind
In sad and subtle chops.
The stars were weary of routine:
The trees in the plantation
Were growing every fruit at once,
In search of a sensation.
The moon went for a moonlight stroll,
And tried to be a bard,
And gazed enraptured at itself:
I left it trying hard.
The sea had nothing but a mood
Of "vague ironic gloom,"
With which t'explain its presence in
My upstairs drawing room.
The sun had read a little book
That struck him with a notion:
He drowned himself and all his fires
Deep in the hissing ocean.
Then all was dark, lawless, and lost:
I heard great devilish wings:
I knew that Art had won, and snapt
The Covenant of Things.[36]

[36] "On the Disastrous Spread of Aestheticism in All Classes," in J. Sullivan, ed., *G. K. Chesterton, Greybeards at Play, and other Comic Verse* (London, 1974), 42-47.

The slogan "art for art's sake" retained its power to elicit from Chesterton occasional expressions of impatience. Thus, in his survey book *The Victorian Age in Literature* he remarks near the outset:

> It is quite needless here to go into the old "art for art's sake" business, or explain at length why individual artists cannot be reviewed without reference to their traditions or creeds. It is enough to say that with other creeds they would have been, for literary purposes, other individuals.[37]

Professional (and Confessional) Beginnings

Given his allergy to mediums and ouija boards, it was ironic that Chesterton's first job on leaving the Slade was for a small Bloomsbury publisher specialising in spiritualism and the occult. He soon got through a backlog of manuscripts submitted, sending them back to, as he put it, "addresses, which I should imagine, must be private asylums."[38] After a few months of this he was able to get a post with a mainstream publisher, T. Fisher Unwin, later taken over by Ernest Benn. Chesterton's courtship of his future wife, Frances Bloggs, the first dogmatico-sacramental Christian he appears to have met (she was an Anglo-Catholic), and the launching of his career as a reviewer in London journals began now, in 1896. By the end of 1900 he was selling articles to London papers on a regular basis.

At this stage — the closing years of the nineteenth century — Chesterton's mind had three comparatively settled components. The first, which he owed in part to his reading of the American

---

[37] *The Victorian Age in Literature*, 8-9.

[38] Cited in M. Ward, *Gilbert Keith Chesterton*, 67.

poet Walt Whitman, but far more to the spontaneous experience of his own childhood, was piety towards the cosmos. "I put great faith in the healing power of the great winds and the sun. 'Nature,' as Walt Whitman says, 'and her primal sanities.' "[39] The cosmic environment of human living would remain one of Chesterton's distinctive preoccupations. (It should be added that Whitman's intoxication with the physical universe of skies and grass also extended to human comradeship, as did that of Chesterton.)

The second component was Socialism, which later yielded to Distributism, notably under the influence of Hilaire Belloc, who was as opposed to Socialism as he was to Capitalism. In his auto-biography, Chesterton explains that he became a Socialist only because it was intolerable not to be, granted the chaotic consequences of over-industrialisation and the increasing penury, with the agrarian depression lasting from the mid 1870s to the mid 1890s, of the rural proletariat.

The third and last component was an increasing sympathy with Christian theism. Such theism was as yet doctrinally unformulated. Its starting-point was what Chesterton registered as a need to give thanks for membership in the cosmos. As he would later put it in *Orthodoxy*, birth itself seemed a birthday present. To whom could one give thanks if not a God? His theism included admiration for the Jesus of the Gospels. It also sought to find a strong affinity between the teaching of Jesus and contemporary Socialism, notably through the role in each of compassion, an assault on covetousness, and what St Paul had called "bearing one another's burdens," which Chesterton interpreted in terms of political economy to mean "leveling, silencing, and reducing one's own chances, for the [sake of the] chance of your weaker brethren." These three

---

[39] Cited in M. Ward, *Gilbert Keith Chesterton*, 110.

elements of self-abnegation were, wrote Chesterton, the "three fountains of collectivist passion," common to Socialists and the New Testament alike.[40]

Thaxted and Merry England

The Chestertons' marriage would be solemnised by the most famous Socialist Anglo-Catholic clergyman in England, Conrad Noel, the vicar of Thaxted in north Essex. Noel's 1906 Church Socialist League, a much more radicalised version of two previous left-wing High Anglican bodies, the 1877 Guild of St Matthew and the 1889 Christian Social Union, advocated a revolutionary overthrow of the existing political, social, and economic order in England by bringing land, heavy industry, and transport into public ownership by all available means, not excluding a general strike or armed insurrection. Noel was a "little Englander" who despised the British Empire as arrogant, parasitical, greedy, and cosmopolitan. Although he supported the First World War as a righteous struggle against German militarism, he also approved of the war-time Easter Rising in Ireland: in his church the Sinn Fein tricolour and the Red Flag were displayed alongside the Cross of St George. His Socialism acknowledged as its closest political neighbor the Marxian "Social Democratic Federation," whose most famous supporter had been the Romantic poet and designer William Morris. Like Morris, Noel wanted to combine Socialist revolution with a revival of native English traditions in arts and crafts, and — especially stressed by Noel — song and dance, which in Thaxted became para-liturgical: forms of festivity following on the elaborate Sarum-rite Eucharists, Corpus Christi processions, and other ceremonies celebrated in the parish church, whose

[40] Ibid., 71-72.

patron, the eccentric Frances Maynard, Countess of Warwick, kept at bay the strongly disapproving bishops of Chelmsford. Although Chesterton began early to have doubts about the interrelatedness of Socialism and Christianity, Noel's influence on him can hardly be overestimated. Chesterton would follow Noel, albeit less "folkloristically," in drawing attention to what Noel's biographer Reg Groves calls

> fragmentary survivals of a past way of life and culture that had once been rooted in popular life; regional and local in inspiration, and so [it might be hoped] ultimately universal in its more profound expressions.[41]

Both men — Noel and Chesterton — sought a unified cultural vision on religious foundations. "My own work," remarked Noel towards the end of his life:

> though poor in languages and scholarship, has been to synthesize and develop the work of many original thinkers and make it more of a unity . . . I believe we hold in the kind of Thaxted theology, philosophy and politics, something that is a development and yet enshrines a huge amount of the truth without which our age must perish.[42]

And he went on to say that the Church's goal is

> revolutionary and political (in a wide sense) but ever so much more. It holds all values of redemption, and has its outlook on drama, on amusements, on crafts and trades, on music, on dancing, on every kind of human activity and

---

[41] R. Groves, *Conrad Noel and the Thaxted Movement: An Adventure in Christian Socialism* (London, 1967), 120.

[42] Ibid., 321.

expressions. Its task is therefore infinitely more difficult and complex than that of cruder, narrower parties like the Communists or the Labour folk . . . I think it holds in embryo in the Gospels, and in greater detail in its best thinking and most living tradition the secret of life for men.[43]

Noel's synthesis of Socialism and Anglo-Catholicism would be mirrored in Chesterton's synthesis of Distributism and Catholicism, first Anglo- and later Roman. The common factors were, at first, the inspiration, both social and aesthetic, of Morris, and later, the role of classical Christian doctrine and morals. But even as Chesterton began to approach the latter, he started to part from the former, as his notebooks bear witness.

Mr. William Morris . . . in his *News from Nowhere* gives a beautiful picture of a land ruled by Love, and rightly grounds the give-and-take camaraderie of his ideal state upon an assumed improvement in human nature. But he does not tell us how such an improvement is to be effected, and Christ did . . . When we compare the spiritual attitudes of two thinkers, one of whom is considering whether social history has been sufficiently a course of improvement to warrant him in believing that it will culminate in universal altruism, while the other is considering whether he loves people enough to walk down tomorrow to the marketplace and distribute everything but his staff and his scrip, it will not be denied that the latter is likely to undergo certain deep and acute emotional experiences, which will be quite unknown to the former.[44]

---

[43] Ibid, 322.
[44] Cited in M. Ward, *Gilbert Keith Chesterton*, 74.

In an admiring yet also critical essay on Morris, Chesterton lauded him in these words:

> Poet of the childhood of nations, craftsman in the new honesties of art, prophet of a merrier and wiser life, his fullblooded enthusiasm will be remembered when human life has once more assumed flamboyant colours and proved that this awful greenish grey of the aesthetic twilight in which we now live is, in spite of all the pessimists, not the greyness of death, but the greyness of dawn.[45]

That generous tribute was paid in 1902. But six years later Chesterton took his definitive leave of Socialism in an article entitled "Why I Am Not a Socialist," published in the distinctly *avant-garde* journal *The New Age*. In the summary offered by Chesterton's biographer Michael Ffinch, with citations from the original:

> Just as imperialism had been foisted upon [the "mass of the common people"] by the interests of commerce and international banking, so socialism would be imposed on them by the interests of intellectuals, "decorative artists and Oxford dons and journalists and Countesses on the spree."[46]

It is difficult not to think that by "decorative artists" Chesterton has in mind Morris, just as the "Countesses" necessarily conjure up Noel's patron, the wife of the Earl of Warwick. Not surprisingly, the second of the two Russian revolutions of 1917 would complete

---

[45] "William Morris," in *Twelve Types: A Book of Essays* (London, 1902), 30.

[46] M. Ffinch, *G. K. Chesterton*, 157, with an internal citation from "Why I Am Not a Socialist," published in *The New Age* for 4 January 1908.

the process of Chesterton's disenchantment, though without ex-
tinguishing his own brand of radicalism. By 1922 he was writing
the following: "Those who will not even admit the Capitalist problem deserve to get the Bolshevist solution. All things considered, I
cannot say anything worse of them than that."[47] This reaction was
not uncommon. A lifelong Anglican Distributist, Maurice Reckitt,
commented wryly:

> [T]he catastrophic achievements of a militant Marxism in
> eastern Europe were suggesting that the word "revolution-
> ary," which Church socialists had been accustomed to employ
> with a somewhat light-hearted vagueness, would require in
> future to be used more circumspectly.[48]

In the early *Notebooks* entry on Morris and Christ, Chesterton added that the "Galilaean programme" at least makes more
provision than does Socialism for what he calls the "real triad of
Christian virtues": humility, activity, and cheerfulness. If upon
hearing those words, dogmatic theologians cannot help feel a
sense of anti-climax, they need to recall that this text comes from
the period before Chesterton discovered doctrinal Christianity.

The first clear evidence for Chesterton's adherence to a dogmatic confession was prompted by a manifesto of rationalism, *God
and My Neighbour*, in which its author, Robert Blatchford, editor
of the journal *The Clarion*, set out his reasons for not being a
Christian. Chesterton's response, published a few months later as
a contribution to a counterblast, *The Doubts of Democracy*, anticipates the line of argument of his mature apologetics, and notably

---

[47] *What I Saw in America*, 127.

[48] M. Reckitt, *Maurice to Temple: A Century of the Social Movement
in the Church of England* (London, 1946), 167.

the second, Christological, section of that two-part work, *The Everlasting Man*, which dates from 1925.[49]

How, then, did that discovery of doctrinal Christianity come about? Like all momentous shifts in outlook, it probably had its conditioning factors, of which the influence and example of his fiancée, later wife, was surely chief (he would dedicate *The Ballad of the White Horse* to the woman who "brought the cross to me"), and that of Noel a good second — as the *Autobiography* can testify.[50] But at root his conversion was the dawning of an intellectual conviction of which Chesterton gives a celebrated account at the opening of his 1908 masterpiece, *Orthodoxy*. The world-view he was developing in personal reaction to the contemporary intelligentsia turned out to be, in key essentials, the same as the ancient faith of the Church. Or, as he had already put it in the essay "The Doubts of Democracy": "If I gave each of my reasons for being a Christian, a vast number of them would be Mr. Blatchford's reasons for not being one."[51]

In the course of writing in 1904 a study of contemporary intellectual trends, under the title *Heretics*, where Blatchford continued to figure, Chesterton found there were a number of Blatchfords of differing kinds. He judged that the reasons for which Christianity was thus attacked from all sides were in many respects contradictory. This was so, he thought, not only in the negative sense of the objectors cancelling each other out but also in the positive sense that their opposite objections pointed to something uniquely balanced and fitting to the human condition in evangelical and

---

[49] Crucial sections of the essay are anthologised in M. Ward, *Gilbert Keith Chesterton*, 172-176.

[50] *Autobiography*, 159-163.

[51] M. Ward, *Gilbert Keith Chesterton*, 172.

catholic orthodoxy — and what a later generation would call "orthopraxy": right practice.

Political Engagements

Chesterton's conversion to a full-blooded Christianity coincided with the journalistic enterprise which made his name in Britain, and that was his campaign against the Second Boer War, a war which pitted the British Empire for reasons commercial and strategic against the two small Afrikaaaner republics, the Transvaal and the Orange Free State, whose white population later in the twentieth century (but not at its opening) would become associated with the notorious system of social relations called "apartheid." Opposition to the Boer War was rife on the radical wing of the Liberal Party, to which at this time Chesterton adhered, but it failed to capture the party as a whole. Indeed, many of the party members — the "Liberal Imperialists" — made common cause with the Conservatives in supporting the war, while the Liberal leader in the Commons, Henry Campbell-Bannerman, abstained at the crucial vote. Chesterton argued for nations with coherent internal cultures over against cosmopolitan empires which deracinated rulers and ruled. In *What I Saw in America* (1922) he would write: "The objection to spreading anything all over the world is that, among other things, you have to spread it very thin."[52] Moreover, he suspected — not without reason — the invisible hand of high finance pulling the strings of government behind the scenes. Yet uppermost in the mind of Lord Salisbury, the Conservative prime minister, was the loss to imperial prestige if British paramountcy in South Africa were successfully defied.[53]

[52] *What I Saw in America*, 244-245.

[53] A. Roberts, *Salisbury: Victorian Titan* (London, 1999, 2000), 714-740.

G. K. Chesterton, Theologian

The Boer crisis brought Chesterton together with a pugnacious fellow-writer, Hilaire Belloc, as classical a stylist as Chesterton was romantic, a Catholic by birth, an historian (of a sort) by his Oxford training, and for a while a Liberal member of Parliament. In the 1910 election, Belloc, angered by what he saw as the Party's turn to a "Welfare State" that was halfway to a "Servile State," stood as an Independent candidate and won. Later, under the administration of David Lloyd George, notorious for what the later twentieth century would call "sleaze," Belloc would abandon with disgust not only the Liberal Party but also modern Parliamentarianism as a whole — and draw Chesterton with him. Though Shaw's term for Belloc and Chesterton jointly, "the Chesterbelloc," hardly does justice to the differences of form and content in their writing, it serves to draw attention to a collaboration. (Their *literal* collaboration consisted in Chesterton's illustrations for a number of Belloc's books.) Chesterton relied on Belloc for, notably, historical knowledge. He was conscious of his lack of background in the older Universities, though hardly apologetic for it; he considered the education Oxford and Cambridge offered undergraduates to be largely a lamentable collusion in the self-indulgent lifestyle of pampered young men: "[I]t is not a working way of managing education to be entirely content with the mere fact that you have given the luckiest boys the jolliest time."[54]

Chesterton was not a pacifist, as his broadsides against the Russian novelist and popular philosopher Leo Tolstoy made plain.

Nothing is baser in our time than the idea that we can have special enthusiasms for things, so long as they are secure,

---

[54] *All Things Considered* (London, 1908), 97.

without pledging ourselves to uphold them if they are ever in peril.[55]

He accepted the necessity of the First World War: the world had to be made safe from Prussian militarism. He did not volunteer; by 1914 his girth was already alarming. A lady on a London street who interrogated him with the words, "Why are you not out at the Front?" was met by his celebrated riposte: "Madame, if you go round to my side, you will see that I am."

The War brought great grief to Chesterton nonetheless. The death of his brother Cecil in a fever hospital in northern France ("trench fever" was a frequent killer in the grim fighting conditions of the Western Front) robbed him of his only surviving sibling. In due course, a curious exchange of gifts took place. Gilbert took over Cecil's journalistic enterprise as editor of what would later become *G. K.'s Weekly*. Cecil passed on his (Roman) Catholic faith. Not, however, quite yet.

Literary Output: the Anglican Phase

By the summer of 1922, when Chesterton was received into the Catholic Church by the priest whom he would immortalise as the fictional detective Father Brown, Chesterton was a major — if controversial — literary figure in England. In addition to some hundreds of articles in newspapers and magazines, many of which remain uncollected, he had published studies of the artists William Blake and George Frederick Watts; of the writers Robert Browning, George Bernard Shaw, and Dickens; as well as a general survey of Victorian literature — all books full of incisive, not to mention provocative, judgements. He had written a

[55] *The Glass Walking-stick and Other Essays*, ed. D. Collins (London, 1955), 71.

short history of England, five fantastic novels,[56] the first sets of Father Brown stories, five books of poetry, and at least a dozen collections of essays,[57] as well as two works crucial for understanding his theological outlook: *Heretics* and *Orthodoxy*, to whose examination I shall be devoting the lion's share of the next two chapters of this book. Chesterton's studies of other creative artists can be ransacked for their insights, including theological, and are not treated as sober historical introductions to their subjects. This is as Chesterton wished. Of his study, *Robert Browning*, he wrote:

> I will not say I wrote a book on Browning; but I wrote a book on love, liberty, poetry, my own views of God and religion (highly developed), and various theories of my own about optimism and pessimism and the hope of the world; a book in which the name of Browning was introduced from time to time, I might almost say with considerable art, or at any rate with some decent appearance of regularity.[58]

The tone here is deliberately self-mocking (T. S. Eliot, for example, thought Chesterton was without rival as a critic of Dickens). In fact, the Browning book led to an invitation to become the first occupant of the Chair of English Literature at the "redbrick" University of Birmingham. Had he accepted, Chesterton

[56] The classic study is I. Boyd, *The Novels of G. K. Chesterton: A Study in Art and Propaganda* (London, 1975).

[57] For an account of the variety of Chesterton's approach to essay writing, against the background of a history of the essay form and with some subtly analysed examples of how Chesterton gained his effects, see J. D. Coates, *G. K. Chesterton as Controversialist, Essayist, Novelist, and Critic* (Lewiston, New York, 2002), 117-155.

[58] *Autobiography*, 95.

would have met the young J.R.R. Tolkien. But perhaps it was as well for academe that he declined: the boundary-lines defining subject-matter were necessarily porous to one who thought that, as Chesterton put it in his study of Watts:

> There is no detail from buttons to kangaroos, that does not enter into the gay confusion of philosophy. There is no fact of life, from the death of a donkey to the General Post Office, which has not its place to dance and sing in, in the glorious Carnival of theology.[59]

One reviewer of the Browning book singled out for praise what I believe to be the heart of Chesterton's wider imaginative achievement, namely, his success in giving the reader "the wild joy of looking upon the world once more for the first time."[60] It is hard to think of much if anything from Chesterton's Anglican period which he needed to jettison on finding a spiritual home elsewhere. All aspects of his copious literary production in the years before 1922 are germane to his standing as a Christian thinker in the Catholic tradition. In succeeding chapters, they are liberally drawn upon in presenting the philosophical and theological themes Chesterton chose to treat — and treat so well that one could imagine some future Pope declaring him a Doctor of the Church.[61]

---

[59] G. F. *Watts* (London, 1904; 1975), p. 75.

[60] Cited in M. Ffinch, G. K. *Chesterton*, 111.

[61] That assumes Chesterton could be acknowledged as an example of Christian holiness of life, something not obviously impossible. The genres of his writing are, of course, atypical of the great Doctors — but much the same could be said of, for example, Thérèse of Lisieux, declared *doctor ecclesiae* by Pope John Paul II in 1997.

G. K. Chesterton, Theologian

Conversion to Rome

Before looking into that imaginative achievement in the body of this book, we need to complete this overview by a retrospect on the (Roman) Catholic period of Chesterton's life. Chesterton's move from Anglo-Catholicism to the Church of Rome was motivated by concern for legitimate authority. After all, this had been the nub of the issue between Jesus and the Jewish leaders of his time: where and how was divine authority to be accessed in historical society? As early as 1909, when the third of Chesterton's novelistic fantasia, *The Ball and the Cross,* was published, with a Highland Catholic as its quasi-hero, rumours had circulated that Chesterton was to convert to the Church of Rome. Shortly after *The Ball and the Cross* appeared, Chesterton discussed his spiritual concerns with two Catholic priests who struck up a conversation with him at Coventry railway station, saying, "It's a matter that is giving me a great deal of agony of mind."[62] The likely effects of such a move on his non-Catholic wife served as a strong deterrent to Chesterton's conversion.

In the last weeks of 1914 Chesterton had suffered a serious stress-induced illness, provoked by his gruelling schedule of lecture engagements and journalists' deadlines, as well as by the court proceedings against his brother Cecil for criminal libel in attacking senior government figures over illicit share-dealing. (Cecil was the editor of *The New Witness,* a paper founded to monitor evidence of corruption in public life.) It was an unhappy period, characterised by some atypically acerbic journalism and a sharpening of his remarks about the nefarious activities, real or imaginary, of Jewish financiers based on the high-level skulduggery of the "Marconi Affair" (1911-1913), of which a very full account is

[62] Cited in M. Ffinch, *G. K. Chesterton,* 183.

given in the biography of Chesterton by Alzina Stone Dale.[63] In this severe medical crisis (for a while he was thought unlikely to recover) his wife Frances was reconciled to summoning Father John O'Connor to receive Chesterton into the Catholic Church by administration of the last sacraments in the event that his condition worsened.[64] In fact Chesterton recovered, and it took another eight years before he steeled himself to make the move without his wife.

Various factors were in play in the temptation to "pope." As Adam Schwartz suggests, Chesterton's visit to the Holy Land in 1919-1920 as a special correspondent for the *Daily Telegraph* may have "heightened his sensibility to Christianity's historicity and the consequent importance of tradition."[65] Again, the Anglican Communion's 1920 Lambeth Conference struck him as flawed by a tendency to doctrinal minimalism, and thus by an openness to accommodation with Modernism.[66] By contrast, the constancy of the Roman teaching office increasingly stood out. Here was a firm point of reference in a changing world and Church. He would write in his study of Chaucer:

> The Church is not a movement or a mood or a direction, but the balance of many movements and moods, and membership of it consists of accepting the ultimate arbitrament which strikes the balance between them.[67]

---

[63] A. S. Dale, *The Outline of Sanity*, 168-183.

[64] M. Ward, *Gilbert Keith Chesterton*, 330.

[65] A. Schwartz, *The Third Spring: G. K. Chesterton, Graham Greene, Christopher Dawson, and David Jones* (Washington 2005), 78. The Jerusalem stay bore fruit in *The New Jerusalem* (London, 1920).

[66] See I. Boyd, C.S.B., "Chesterton's Anglican Reaction to Modernism," in A. Nichols, O.P., ed., *Chesterton and the Modernist Crisis* (Saskatoon, 1990), 5-36.

[67] *Chaucer: A Study* (London, 1932), 341.

But above all the sacramental authority of the Catholic Church to renew baptismal rebirth by absolution from sins occupied the forefront of his mind. It meant for him spiritual resurrection. As he put it in the sestet of the sonnet he wrote on his reception into the Church:

> *The sages have a hundred maps to give*
> *That trace their crawling cosmos like a tree,*
> *They rattle reason out through many a sieve*
> *That stores the sand and lets the gold go free:*
> *And all these things are less than dust to me*
> *Because my name is Lazarus and I live.*[68]

Six months later he explained his decision in intellectually wider terms to his fellow-convert, the writer Maurice Baring, who seems to have been, one can note in passing, the original of Horne Fisher, the hero of a novel of high politics Chesterton had just published, *The Man Who Knew Too Much.*[69] As Chesterton wrote to Baring:

That there has always been [in the Church of England] a High Church Party is true; that there has always been an Anglo-Catholic Party may be true, but I am not so sure of it . . . But there is one matter arising from that which I do think important. Even the High Church Party, even the Anglo-Catholic Party only confronts a particular heresy called Protestantism upon particular points . . . If [High Anglicanism] is not the heresy of an age, at least it is only the anti-heresy of an

---

[68] *Collected Poems* (London, 1933), 387.

[69] *The Man Who Knew Too Much* (London, 1922). For the plausible identification of Horne Fisher with Baring, see I. Boyd, *The Novels of G. K. Chesterton*, 79-83.

age. But since I have been a Catholic, I am conscious of being in a much vaster arsenal, full of arms against countless other potential enemies. The Church, as the Church and not merely as ordinary opinion, has something to say to philosophies which the merely High Church has never had occasion to think about.[70]

He would take such thoughts further in *The Catholic Church and Conversion*, published following his wife's reception into the Faith in 1926.

Literary Output: the Catholic Phase

In the remaining years of his life (he died on 14 June 1936), Chesterton himself had many things to say about some of those philosophies. He remained much in demand as a public speaker, even if his capacity to turn up at the right place at the right time was notoriously deficient — witness the celebrated telegram to his wife: "Am in Market Harborough, where ought I to be?" He made a speaking tour of the United States in 1930-1931, repeating the success he had achieved in an earlier visit in 1920, where he risked such remarks as these in Chicago: "I do not plan to go farther west than Chicago, for having seen Jerusalem and Chicago, I think I shall have touched the extremes of civilization."[71] He also spent three months in Rome, staying with his wife, Frances, and his secretary (later, literary executor) Dorothy Collins, at the famous Hotel Hassler, at the top of the Spanish Steps. The visit included meetings with Pope Pius XI and Mussolini. He was more impressed with the latter than he expected, though he concluded

---

[70] Cited in M. Ward, *Gilbert Keith Chesterton*, 390.
[71] Cited A. S. Dale, *The Outline of Sanity*, 225.

his account of modern Italy confessing that "by every instinct of my blood, I . . . prefer English liberty to Latin discipline."[72]

His literary output during this post-conversion period did not diminish. From his Catholic period, we have studies of Chaucer, the Scots novelist Robert Louis Stevenson and the early-nineteenth-century social critic William Cobbett; hagiography — his books on Francis of Assisi and Thomas Aquinas; some twenty essay collections; an autobiography (to be posthumously published), two plays, more poems and Father Brown stories, and the principal theological work of his life, *The Everlasting Man*. Again, there are hundreds of uncollected magazine articles, above all from his re-launching of *The New Witness* as *G. K.'s Weekly*, in an effort to render viable a paper which had languished since his brother's death at the end of the last Western Front campaign of the First World War. In the 1930s he gained a new audience through BBC radio, his high-pitched but beautifully modulated voice well-suited to this medium.[73]

Typical themes of Chesterton's maturity were the imaginative and argumentative defence of historic Christianity in its dogmas, practices, and saints, Distributism (in 1926 *G. K.'s Weekly* became the official mouthpiece of the Distributive League, and Chesterton the League's President[74]), and, most fundamental of all, the thesis that man was not merely an animal who had evolved from a primitive life-form but a special creation, in the image of God.

---

[72] *The Resurrection of Rome* (London, 1930), 283.

[73] A. S. Dale, *The Outline of Sanity*, 288.

[74] Some major articles of Chesterton on Distributism from *G. K.'s Weekly* were published in 1926 as *The Outline of Sanity* — which should not be confused, of course, with the biography of the same title by A. S. Dale in the previous footnote.

Though not all Chesterton's biographers approve, his own *Autobiography* ends, in fact, with the affirmation that his reception into the Catholic Church was absolutely decisive for him: "[T]his overwhelming conviction that there is one key which can unlock all doors brings back to me my first glimpse of the glorious gift of the senses; and the sensational experience of sensation . . ."[75] Chesterton had sought to recapture this "glimpse" in *Orthodoxy* and elsewhere, and he registers, in the book's closing words, a curious correspondence between a figure in his father's toy-theatre and the Peter whose vicar is the pope of Rome.

> [T]here starts up again before me, standing sharp and clear in shape as of old, the figure of a man who crosses a bridge and who carries a key; as I saw him when I first looked into fairyland through the window of my father's peep-show. But I know that he who is called Pontifex, the Builder of the Bridge, is called also Claviger, the Bearer of the Key; and that such keys were given him to bind and loose when he was a poor fisher in a far province, beside a small and almost secret sea.[76]

Still, other Christians, beyond the confines of the Catholic Church, can appreciate what I am calling in this book Chesterton's *theology* since, as Dorothy L. Sayers, herself an Anglican, wrote of him in her preface to *The Surprise*:

> To the young people of my generation, G. K. C. was a kind of Christian liberator. Like a beneficent bomb, he blew out of the Church a quantity of stained glass of a very bad

---

[75] *Autobiography*, 355.

[76] Ibid.

period, and let in gusts of fresh air, in which the dead leaves of doctrine danced with all the energy and indecorum of Our Lady's Tumbler.[77]

In his copy, given him by the author, of Sir Oliver Lodge's *The Substance of Faith Allied with Science: A Catechism for Parents and Teachers*, by the side of the question, "What is the duty of man?" Chesterton pencilled in his own answer: "To love God mystically and his neighbour as himself."[78] Let that, then, be his epitaph.

[77] D. L. Sayers, Preface, *The Surprise* (London, 1952).

[78] O. Lodge, *The Substance of Faith Allied with Science: A Catechism for Parents and Teachers* (London, 1907), 129. I thank Mr Stratford Caldecott of the Chesterton Library in Oxford for showing me this item in the collection of Chesterton's own holdings.

Chapter 2

Chesterton and the Edwardian Cultural Crisis

Chesterton sought to affirm timeless truths, either about the human condition or about Christian revelation: truths that would be, as we might say nowadays, cross-cultural and intergenerational in span. But he himself wrote from out of a very definite cultural conjuncture, into which he was closely bound by his life as a journalist. I am taking a leaf out of a book by Professor John Coates of the University of Hull which makes this very point when I call this chapter "Chesterton and the Edwardian Cultural Crisis."[79]

I find myself easily persuaded by Coates's essential thesis, namely, that there was in the Edwardian period a sharply increased intellectual and moral instability among the educated class in England, and, moreover, that Chesterton registered this crisis with particular acuteness, since he was alarmed by its negative implications, though he also saw the positive possibilities for a clarification of issues. I am doubtful, though, about Coates's further claim that when Chesterton wrote *Heretics*, the most obvious

[79] J. D. Coates, *Chesterton and the Edwardian Cultural Crisis, passim.* Many of the themes are taken further in idem., G. K. *Chesterton as Controversialist, Essayist, Novelist, and Critic.*

book-length source for his view of the contemporary intellectual life, the "crisis" was in a merely embryonic stage in which it consisted more of confusion than of error. Only in the latter part of the quite short reign of Edward VII, thinks Coates, and notably with the fuller English reception, after 1906, of the writings of Friedrich Nietzsche, did Chesterton realise that more than muddle was at stake.[80] In 1906, as we shall see, Chesterton was already hot on the trail of the Nietzschean *Übermensch*. That did not have to await *Orthodoxy*, the sequel to *Heretics*, in 1908, or the publication of Chesterton's book on the Anglo-Irish playwright George Bernard Shaw, a late convert to Nietzscheanism, in 1910.

Secular Heresies as Negative Indicators of the Truth

It is worth asking what Chesterton thought was wrong with his age because his analysis of its ills will prove to be crucial for his presentation of the Christian Gospel, in all three key respects of that Gospel's central claims, its background presuppositions, and its further implications. It was when reviewers of *Heretics* challenged him to come clean about what he considered the antithesis to "heresies" that he set out to write *Orthodoxy* and in doing so made plain he had rediscovered the Christian religion. In various ways, the different heresies he had described in *Heretics* constituted, that is, negative indicators of the truth of revelation. He had found in the positions of Kipling, Shaw, Wells, Ibsen, Tolstoy,

---

[80] "Confusion" may have been more the ethos of the 1890s. It is dangerous to build too much on one citation but one notes how, asked about the aims of the *Yellow Book* project, its editors, Aubrey Beardsley and Henry Harland, replied it would contain "clever stuff"and be distinctively "modern," though neither was able to say what "modern" meant. Thus, J. G. Nelson, *The Early Nineties: A View from the Bodley Head* (Cambridge, Massachusetts, 1971), 299.

and other, less well known, writers in favour with the Edwardian intelligentsia, certain anthropological errors. When these errors were contradicted *en bloc*, the truths asserted formed a pattern, so Chesterton found, and that pattern of *Orthodoxy* turned out to be nothing other than the template the Church had always offered to thought. As David Fagerberg has put it, at the time of writing *Heretics* Chesterton was "learning Christianity by a sort of *via negativa*,"[81] to which, we can add, *Orthodoxy* is the cataphatic completion, on a *via affirmativa* all Chesterton's own. *Heretics* is, then, a key book in Chesterton's *oeuvre*, and he intended *Orthodoxy* to be read in conjunction with it: these are complementary volumes in a two-part work.

Woolly-mindedness:
"A total levity on the subject of cosmic philosophy"

Chesterton's "introductory remarks" in *Heretics* confirm that when he set out to write this book, he was as much exercised by other people's allergy to reflection as he was anxious about any disastrous trains of thought ill-conceived reflection might prompt. Thus far Coates is correct. In 1906 Chesterton was worried by what he called a "total levity on the subject of cosmic philosophy."[82] People, he observed, are encouraged to discuss details in art, politics, literature, to have an opinion about tram-cars or Botticelli. A man, "may turn over and explore a million objects," he lamented, "but he must not find that strange object, the universe; for if he does he will have a religion, and be lost. Everything matters — except everything."[83]

---

[81] D. Fagerberg, *The Size of Chesterton's Catholicism* (Notre Dame, Indiana, 1998), 8.

[82] *Heretics* (London, 1906, 2006), 2.

[83] Ibid.

G. K. Chesterton, Theologian

In an early example of his so-called love of paradox, Chesterton finds that there was more real liberty in a regime of inquisitorial censorship in the ages of faith than there is under modern liberalism. As he explains, "[t]he old restriction meant that only the orthodox were allowed to discuss religion. Modern liberty means that nobody is allowed to discuss it,"[84] since to do so offends against good taste. Chesterton begs to differ, citing his conviction that "the most practical and important thing about a man is still his view of the universe."

What is objectionable in contemporary culture, according to Chesterton, is the lack of any serious consideration of what he calls "general theories of the relation of things."[85] Such theories have been excluded from literature by the cry of "art for art's sake." The artist need not bother about the fate of humanity, the aesthetician Clive Bell would declare in 1914, since "aesthetic rapture is self-justifying."[86] Chesterton would reply some years later: "I would rather have no art at all than one which occupies itself in matching shades of peacock and turquoise for a decorative scheme of blue devils."[87] General theories of the relation of things have likewise been replaced in politics, so Chesterton complained, by concern with efficiency. In the 1890s, "National Efficiency" became the slogan of the group of lobbyists from Conservative, Liberal, and Socialist backgrounds who jointly advocated a "willingness to

---

[84] *Heretics*, 2.

[85] Ibid., 4.

[86] C. Bell, *Art* (London, 1914), 241.

[87] *A Gleaming Cohort* (London, 1926), 184. He wrote decisively four years later: "All art is religious . . . Religion is the sense of ultimate reality, of whatever meaning a man finds in his own existence, or the existence of anything else": *Come to Think of It* (London, 1930), 64.

use government power to organize and legislate for an 'Imperial race' fit to meet the challenges of the world."[88] Chesterton had evidently registered the intellectually amorphous character of such statements. Without a general view of the goal of politics in its relation to all other human things, such concern for national efficiency would be itself supremely inefficient.

Heretics *on the Contemporary* "*Negative Spirit*"

In the chapter that follows his introduction to *Heretics*, Chesterton inveighs against what he terms the environing "negative spirit." In *The Victorian Age in Literature* he would describe it as "a curious cold air of emptiness and real subconscious agnosticism such as is extremely unusual in the history of mankind,"[89] and he ascribes it to the mutual destruction of English Christianity and philosophical liberalism in their mid-nineteenth-century disputes. As he explains:

> Liberalism (in Newman's sense) really did strike Christianity through headpiece and head; that is, it did daze and stun the ignorant and ill-prepared English Christian. And Christianity did smite Liberalism through breastplate and through breast; that is, it did succeed, through aims and all sorts of awful accidents, in piercing more or less to the heart of the Utilitarian — and finding that he had none.[90]

The "years that followed on that double disillusionment," Chesterton went on:

---

[88] C. Harvie and H.C.G. Matthew, *Nineteenth Century Britain: A Very Short Introduction* (Oxford, 2000), 128.

[89] *The Victorian Age in Literature*, 215.

[90] Ibid., 214.

were like one long afternoon in a rich house on a rainy day. It was not merely that everybody believed that nothing would happen; it was also that everybody believed that anything happening was even duller than nothing happening.[91]

Chesterton is looking back at the last years of Victoria's reign as well as looking around at immediately contemporary writing when he remarks that modern morality can point to numerous imperfections, while the very concept of positive perfection is lacking. The great gap in modern ethics is any substantive account of how a human being reaches his full flourishing. Translated into the idiom of imaginative literature, there is an "absence of vivid pictures of purity and spiritual triumph."[92] The typically later-nineteenth-century realism of the Norwegian dramatist Henrik Ibsen, extremely popular in Edwardian England, is symptomatic here. Chesterton writes of such realism:

[W]hile the eye that can perceive what are the wrong things increases in an uncanny and devouring clarity, the eye which sees what things are right is growing mistier and mistier every moment, till it goes almost blind with doubt.[93]

Ibsen is decisive against anything he identifies as a root of evil, but vague about what constitutes either virtue or wisdom: what the Scholastics would call the moral and the intellectual virtues respectively. We shall see in a later chapter that Chesterton is a very early example of what became known by the late twentieth century as "virtue ethics." Chesterton points out how Shaw, in his study *The Quintessence of Ibsenism*, sums up Ibsen's message

[91] *The Victorian Age in Literature*, 217.

[92] *Heretics*, 12.

[93] Ibid., 13.

approvingly in words Chesterton cited a number of times in order to pick them apart in different contexts: "The golden rule is that there is no golden rule."[94] This omission of any positive concept of human flourishing or perfection, remarks Chesterton, leaves us "face to face with the problem of a human consciousness filled with very definite images of evil, and with no definite image of good." He continues:

> To us, as to Milton's devils in Pandemonium, it is darkness that is visible. The human race, according to religion [Chesterton goes on], fell once, and in falling gained knowledge of good and evil. Now we have fallen a second time, and only the knowledge of evil remains to us.[95]

The search for the "right life," the "good man" — or the good for man — has been abandoned.

Chesterton will find the novelist and early practitioner of science fiction H. G. Wells a further example of the negative spirit. In *Mankind in the Making* (1903), Wells identified parenthood as the single most important human function. He would not be discussing, he explained, what made people great saints or great heroes but only what made them good fathers and mothers. That sounds sensible until one realises it is, in Chesterton's words, "another example of unconscious shirking." He asks: "What is the good of begetting a man until we have settled what is the good of being a man? You are merely handing on to him a problem you dare not settle yourself."[96] On this agnostic view, the most ethicists can do is put up a few notice-boards at certain points to

---

[94] Ibid., 14.

[95] Ibid.

[96] Ibid., 16.

warn people of obvious dangers, such as: do not drink yourself to death.

But the most egregious example of such minimalist agnosticism is found for Chesterton in the late-Victorian/early-Edwardian cult of progress. Chesterton complains that:

> We meet every ideal of religion, patriotism, beauty, or brute pleasure with the alternative ideal of progress — that is to say, we meet every proposal of getting something that we know about, with an alternative proposal of getting a great deal more of nobody knows what.[97]

For Chesterton, the language of progress, when used in counter-position to definable moral ideals, is patently absurd. As he asserts, "Nobody has any business to use the word 'progress' unless he has a definite creed and a cast-iron code of morals."[98] Without some fixed standard, it is not possible to make a judgment as to whether value is increasing or decreasing, whether there is progress or re-gress in human affairs.

So far, then, into *Heretics* Chesterton confirms Coates's claim that the principal malaise of his age is indeed woolly-mindedness — combined with "negative spirit." But what happens to that claim when Chesterton explores individual heresies?

Chesterton on Kipling and Rhodes

The first of these individual heresies comes labelled Rudyard Kipling. Chesterton's hostility to imperialism made it pretty inevi-table that Kipling would come high on his list for criticism, for the subtleties in Kipling's attitude to (above all) India and the British

---

[97] *Heretics*, 16.
[98] Ibid., 17.

remained to be registered in the critical consciousness.[99] That Chesterton's anti-imperialism was honed in his commentary on the Boer War makes it similarly likely that he would add the name of the adventurer-*cum*-empire-builder Cecil Rhodes as a pendant to that of Kipling. Chesterton does not accuse Rhodes and Kipling of a confusion of outlook on the universe. He accuses them, rather, of an erroneous sense of what constitutes magnitude in Rhodes's case, and of what constitutes identity in Kipling's. On *magnitude*, he calls Rhodes, who added many thousands of square miles to the British empire in the countries now called Zambia and Zimbabwe (but then named Rhodesia after him) "a man with singularly small views." As Chesterton writes, "There is nothing large about painting the map red; it is an innocent game for children."[100] To conquer ancient cultures and life-ways is not to have them; it is precisely to lose them.

As for Kipling: Kipling admires England but for quite the wrong reason, namely "because she is strong, not because she is English."[101] "Mr Kipling," writes Chesterton, here raising the flag for local identity,

> knows England as an intelligent gentleman knows Venice. He has been to England a great many times; he has stopped there for long visits. But he does not belong to it, or to any place; and the proof of it is this, that he thinks of England as a place. The more we are rooted in a place, the place vanishes. We live like a tree with the whole strength of the universe.[102]

---

[99] By the mid-1920s, Chesterton was more nuanced on this point, though not fully convinced: thus *The Victorian Age in Literature*, 249.

[100] *Heretics*, 28.

[101] Ibid., 25.

[102] Ibid., 26. This was also the view of Chesterton's younger contemporary, the novelist E. M. Forster: "The imperialist is not what he

Imperialism à la Kipling encourages globe-trotting cosmopolitan-ism, a "motor-car civilization" that sees all and yet sees nothing. Chesterton predicts its exploratory expansionist spirit will lead it to "roar on" at last to "the capture of the solar system, only to find the sun cockney and the stars suburban."[103]

Chesterton on Shaw (plus Schopenhauer and Nietzsche)

Chesterton's criticism of Shaw is more that of unpacking a def-initely false ideology, rather than simply drawing attention to an absence of ideology. In *Heretics* Chesterton goes out of his way to praise Shaw for his clarity of thought and expression. And yet in contrast with the 1910 book on Shaw, which runs for 170 pages be-fore the reader is introduced to Shaw's late acquired Nietzsche-anism, one does not read six pages of the chapter in *Heretics* before he begins to hear of Shaw's "new master," Nietzsche with his the-ory of the *Übermensch*, the Overman or Superman. "He who had to all appearances mocked at the faiths in the forgotten past discov-ered a new god in the unimaginable future."[104] On Chesterton's analysis, Shaw's problem is that he cannot celebrate human be-ings as they are — not just messy but often uproariously messy: he wants them to be rationalistic, pacifist, teetotal, and vegetarian. The 1914 fantasy *The Flying Inn* can be seen as Chesterton's even-tual novelistic response to Shavianism. As Coates notes,

> Nominally about a pub threatened with closure under Na-tional prohibition, *The Flying Inn* deals with the threat to

thinks or seems. He is a destroyer. He prepares the way for cosmo-politanism and though his ambitions may be fulfilled, the earth that he inherits will be gray": *Howard's End* ([1910] Harmonds-worth, 1983), 315.

[103] *Heretics*, 29.

[104] Ibid., 34.

moral choice, existing human nature and the pleasures, idiosyncracies and quiddity of particular existence posed by a "higher" spirituality or by reformers and idealists convinced they know better than the mass of mankind how life should be lived. [105]

In *The Flying Inn*, before the fanatical Lord Ivywood wins the Parliamentary vote to introduce Prohibition, his cousin Dorian Wimpole warns him:

> [Y]ou are in deeper waters than you know. *You* will abolish ale! *You* will make Kent forget hop-poles and Devonshire forget cider! . . . Remember the sensible little High Church curate, who when asked for a Temperance Sermon preached on the text "Suffer us not to be overwhelmed in the water-floods."[106]

To Chesterton's mind, the reason for Shaw's impatience is that he consistently compares the run of people unfavourably to something they are not — whether in the past, where Shaw admires such exceptional figures as the Stoics and Julius Caesar, or in the present, where he applauds the Fabian Society's "economic man," or, so it now emerges, in the future, where Nietzsche's Superman will reign. There is a family resemblance between Chesterton's critique of the worship of size and strength among the imperialists — Kipling and Rhodes — and his attack on Nietzsche's admiration for the "will to power." According to Chesterton, "the greater and stronger a man is, the more he would be inclined to prostrate before a periwinkle,"[107]

[105] J. D. Coates, G. K. *Chesterton as Controversialist, Novelist, Essayist, and Critic*, 77-78.

[106] *The Flying Inn* (London, 1914), 200-201.

[107] *Heretics*, 35.

a humble flowering weed of the hedgerow. The ground for saying so is that the most potent appreciation of reality rests on a "certain mystery of humility." In Chesterton's macarism, adding to the beatitudes pronounced by Christ, "Blessed is he that expecteth nothing, for he shall be gloriously surprised."[108] Shaw, lacking humility, fails to appreciate common humanity with its "warts and all."

In the book-length study of Shaw which followed four years later, Chesterton took the matter further. Chesterton praises Shaw for what he takes to be his typically Irish qualities (his asceticism, though Chesterton was not likely to follow Shaw in this, declaring "there is no natural limit to this rush and riotous gallop of refinement");[109] his intellectual clarity which leads him not to shirk any battle of ideas; and his assumption that political debate is about principles rather than, as Chesterton writes (commenting on the English party system before the Great War), "concerned with which of two wealthy cousins in the same governing class shall be allowed to bring in the same Parish Councils Bill."[110]

At the same time, Chesterton identifies Shaw as a typical Puritan. Born in Dublin in what Chesterton saw as the garrison world

---

[108]*Heretics*, 36.

[109]*George Bernard Shaw* (London, 1910), 25.

[110]Ibid., 32. It might be more accurate to say "before 1912" (rather than 1914), since the introduction of a Liberal bill for Home Rule for Ireland — the price that had to be paid for support by Irish Nationalist MPs for the 1910 reform bill of the House of Lords — brought to the leadership of the Conservatives a politician, Andrew Bonar Law, who vowed the destruction of the Liberal Party. See G. Dangerfield, *The Damnable Question* (London and Boston, 1976). The creation of Lloyd George's Liberal-Conservative coalition government at the Armistice in one sense vindicated Chesterton's perception of the pre-1912 system, a claim reflected in the 1922 novel *The Man Who Knew Too Much*. But it also destroyed the Liberals as a governing Party.

of Protestant Unionism, Shaw was cut off from a wider human environment which could have taught him things, simply because it was closer to the earth, to a motherland, to the domestic. As Chesterton mused, "that he is not rooted in the ancient sagacities of infancy has, I think, a great deal to do with his position as a member of an alien minority in Ireland."[111] Chesterton records that when Shaw was invited to Stratford-on-Avon for the tercentenary of the birth of Shakespeare, he

> wrote back with characteristic contempt: "I do not keep my own birthday, and I cannot see why I should keep Shakespeare's." I think that if Mr Shaw had always kept his own birthday he would be better able to understand Shakespeare's birthday — and Shakespeare's poetry.[112]

For Shaw had notoriously attacked Shakespeare as overrated. In short, Chesterton ascribes to Shaw's Protestant Irish background what he calls his "inhumane humanism," a characteristic he shares, so Chesterton feels, with Shaw's fellow-countryman Dean Swift.

Shaw's Puritanism means, however, more than that. In Ulster one will find, says Chesterton, "the cult of theological clarity combined with barbarous external simplicity."[113] Such Puritanism, which for a period in the seventeenth century enjoyed a cultural hegemony in England, has gradually decayed, not, writes Chesterton:

> because of the advance of modern thought (which means nothing), but because of the slow revival of the mediaeval

[111]*George Bernard Shaw*, 37.
[112]Ibid., 38.
[113]*George Bernard Shaw*, 45.

> energy and character . . . The English were always hearty and humane, and they have made up their minds to be hearty and humane in spite of the Puritans.[114]

All that is left of Puritanism in England is a habit of vague but elevated speech in public life; but in Shaw there remains far more: the Puritan scorn for frivolity, the Puritan disdain for humour as distinct from wit, and the Puritan unwillingness to take a holiday, however short, from responsibility. Without necessarily mentioning Shaw, Chesterton's *Orthodoxy* will need to explain why Shaw is in these regards wrong-headed or wrong-hearted.

The Puritan Irishman is, finally, a Progressive. From the negative animadversions Chesterton has made elsewhere on the cult of progress we shall not expect this to be a compliment. He distinguishes sharply between Progressivism on the one hand and concern with reform on the other. The movement of reform in European (including British) civil life from the French Revolution to the mid-nineteenth century was at its best commendable and worthwhile inasmuch as it had sought measures that were not only concrete but limited, since it is typical of the reformer to identify specifiable ills. The Progressivist, by contrast, asks, What can I alter? As Chesterton puts it:

> The republican temple, like any other strong building, rested on certain definite limits and supports. But the modern man inside it went on indefinitely knocking holes in his own house and saying that they were windows.[115]

Shaw had made the mistake of being "on the insurgent side in everything," of "gnawing at the necessary pillars of all possible society."[116]

---

[114]*George Bernard Shaw*, 44.

[115]Ibid., 62.

[116]Ibid., 73.

Chesterton and the Edwardian Cultural Crisis

There is in Shaw a massive displacement of appropriate attitudes, signalled above all for Chesterton by Shaw's attitude towards
animals and also by his Socialism, from which Chesterton was by
now well distanced. Shaw wished animals to be treated as well as
human beings: "He would waste himself to a white-haired shadow
to save a shark in an aquarium from inconvenience or to add any
little comforts to the life of a carrion-crow." Yet Chesterton reports an inability to identify any occasion where Shaw has uttered
"a single word of tenderness or intimacy with any bird or beast."[117]
Likewise, his Socialism is animated by a wonderful zeal for the
salus populi, the health and welfare of the people, which has led
him to master piles of useful statistics about boring but important
matters. But Shaw has no feeling for ordinary working people as
such, as is evidenced in his own assertion: "I have never had any
feelings about the English working classes except a desire to abol-
ish them and replace them with sensible people."[118] To Chesterton, for whom working-class culture housed certain insights about
features of the human condition vital to a sane anthropology, this
assessment was wide of the mark. Later he would praise William
Cobbett — in words clearly condemning Shavian anthropology
— for differing from "many modern social reformers and from
most modern philanthropists," in his concern "[n]ot merely . . .
with what is called the welfare of the workers. He was very much

[117]Ibid., 78.

[118]Cited in *George Bernard Shaw*, 86. This was not an attitude confined to Shaw. In George Gissing's *Demos: A Story of English
Socialism*, Hubert Eldon expresses the authorial view when he describes English Socialism as irredeemably vulgar, "like everything originating with the English lower classes," *Demos*, vol. III
(London, 1886), 13, cited in J. Carey, *The Intellectuals and the
Masses: Pride and Prejudice Among the Literary Intelligentsia 1880-
1939* (London, 1992), 112.

concerned for their dignity, their good name, their honour, and even their glory."[119]

So far as Shaw's wider philosophy is concerned, Chesterton presents it as a transition from a reworked Schopenhauer to a largely intact Nietzsche. This is out of the frying pan into the fire. For Schopenhauer, author of *The World as Will and Representation*, "[t]he intellect, if it could be impartial, would tell us to cease; but a blind partiality, an instinct quite distinct from thought, drives us on to take desperate chances in an essentially bankrupt lottery."[120] In Shavian terms, life is a higher preoccupation than reason. But Chesterton objects that Shaw's "worship of life" is not itself "lively."[121] "To live" is for Shaw a command of nature which is to be obeyed more than enjoyed. Shaw follows the banner of life austerely, not with joy.

> He paints life at its darkest and then tells the babe unborn to take the leap into the dark . . . It is awful to think that this world which so many poets have praised has even for a time been depicted as a man-trap into which we may just have the manhood to jump. Think of all those ages through which men have talked of having the courage to die. And

---

[119] *William Cobbett* (London, 1925), 45. This attitude lies behind the opposition of Cecil Chesterton's *The Eye-Witness* (the earlier title of *The New Witness*) to Lloyd George's National Insurance Bill. By making it mandatory for all workers between the ages of 16 and 70 to contribute to such insurance, supervised by State commissioners, the legislation would produce a servile working class. Belloc proposed instead voluntary contributions to a programme paid for by a tax chargeable to employers: thus J. P. Corrin, *G. K. Chesterton and Hilaire Belloc: The Battle Against Modernity* (Athens, Ohio; and London, 1981), 49-50.

[120] *George Bernard Shaw*, 193.

[121] Ibid., 194.

then remember that we have actually fallen to talking about having the courage to live.[122]

When Shaw replaced Schopenhauer with Nietzsche as his prime philosophical mentor, he failed to take from Nietzsche the one healthful doctrine the latter could have given him, which was, in Chesterton's estimation, the primacy of delight, valorously attained, over against a merely utilitarian morality.

Christianity, too, believes, remarks Chesterton, somewhat vatically, in "an ultimate and absolute pleasure, not indirect or utilitarian, the intoxication of the spirit, the wine of the blood of God."[123]

What Chesterton means by that is deification, *theosis*: final human fulfilment as gracious participation in the stupefying vision of God. But in the 1903 play *Man and Superman*, together with its accompanying collection of Nietzschean aphorisms, *The Revolutionist's Handbook*, Shaw made it crystal clear which of Nietzsche's doctrines he had in fact taken — and it was not that. The explanation of his selection of the teaching on the *Übermensch* lies for Chesterton in the sudden breaking of one of the "legs of the tripod" (as he puts it) on which Shaw — Irishman, Puritan, Progressive — was sitting. It was the leg of progress that snapped. In Chesterton's explanation of the collapse, Shaw discovered that Plato was a more advanced mind than Shakespeare. As a consequence, Shaw suddenly ceased to believe in educational progress. The man of the future will not be taught. He will be *bred*. Just as the ape produced *homo sapiens*, so *homo sapiens* must now seek to produce something higher than man. The development of this higher being is the purpose of history.

[122]Ibid., 195-196.
[123]Ibid., 205.

G. K. Chesterton, Theologian

In his 1908 essay, "How I Found the Superman," reprinted in the 1910 collection *Alarms and Discursions*, Chesterton parodies Shaw's main source for his knowledge of Nietzsche, the studies by A. R. Orage which gave the English reading public a reasonably fair account of Nietzsche's thought for the first time.[124] Orage had asked rhetorically, "Will the Superman be a man?" and replied to his own question: "Not man as we know him." Chesterton continued in this vein:

> Is the Superman good-looking? "On his own plane," answers the proud father. "Has he any hair?" "Well, not of course what we call hair . . ." "Is it hair or feathers?" "Not feathers, as we understand feathers," answered Hagg in an awful voice.[125]

Moreover, Chesterton considered that "Nietzscheites," as he described them, had failed to answer the question, if the Superman is not simply an exemplification of the highest human ethos as we know it, then why should we desire him anyway?[126]

Chesterton on H. G. Wells

In 1905, H. G. Wells published a book entitled *A Modern Utopia*. Chesterton's positive response to Nietzsche on valour and delight is pertinent to his essay in *Heretics* on Wells, for whom Utopia is to be created by the natural sciences, not by the Superman (though Chesterton notes that Wells's 1904 fantasy *The Food of the Gods and How It Came to Earth* is "Supermannish" in tendency).

[124] A. R. Orage, *Friedrich Nietzsche: The Dionysian Spirit of the Age* (London, 1906); idem., *Nietzsche in Outline and Aphorism* (London, 1907).

[125] Cited in J. Coates, *Chesterton and the Edwardian Cultural Crisis*, 40.

[126] *George Bernard Shaw*, 207.

Leaving Shaw aside now, and taking up Chesterton's critique of Wells, one can see Chesterton suggesting that the spirit of the old Christendom was one of "holding ourselves lightly and yet ready for an infinity of unmerited triumphs."[127] That spirit – which may also be called Nietzsche's at his infrequent best — did fuller justice to humankind than could Wells's hope for a scientific Utopia, because it recognised at one and the same time the essentially flawed nature of human psychology (thus, "holding ourselves lightly," but Wells's rejection of Original Sin blinds him to this) and yet the possibility inherent in human freedom of rising victorious over all that drags us down (thus, "yet ready for an infinity of unmerited triumphs," but Wells's rejection of grace disables him from making this assertion). Writes Chesterton: "The weakness of all Utopias is this, that they take the greatest difficulty of man and assume it to be overcome, and then give an elaborate account of the overcoming of the smaller ones."[128] Given the nature of Chesterton's criticisms of Nietzsche and Shaw, his account of Wells in *Heretics* is surprisingly mild. In the 1901 *Anticipations of the Reaction of Mechanical and Scientific Progress upon Human Life*, Wells had predicted that the rightfully ascendant nation of the future will be, in his words, the one that "most resolutely picks over, educates, sterilizes, exports, or poisons its People of the Abyss," alias the "great useless masses of people."[129] Inspired by the early-nineteenth-century theorist of population Thomas Malthus and by Darwinism, the ethical system in Wells's "New Republic" combines eugenics with the disposal of people who have shown themselves unfit to live through

---

[127]*Heretics*, 39.

[128]Ibid., 45.

[129]H. G. Wells, *Anticipations of the Reaction of Mechanical and Scientific Progress upon Human Life* (London, 1901), 211-212.

the administration of opiates. There is an oblique reference to this view in Chesterton's early novel *The Ball and the Cross*. Professor Lucifer, alias the Devil, shows Turnbull, a humane rationalist, the outcome of secular revolution in a dream sequence that includes the elimination of the unemployable. Lucifer responds to Turnbull's indignant outburst that surely people have rights: "Yes, indeed. Life is sacred — but lives are not sacred. We are improving Life by removing lives."[130] By 1903 in *Mankind in the Making*, Wells had apparently abandoned this programme of enforced or assisted suicide, and likewise decided that eugenics was as yet impractical given the still imperfect character of the science of genetics.

His answer now to the problem of the masses was birth control: in a well-ordered State, parenthood would be restricted to those with the money and intelligence to be responsible rearers of children. Chesterton explains that he is inclined to be merciful to Wells because at least Wells is willing to change his mind. Indeed, Wells often changed his mind but not frequently for the better. In *A Modern Utopia* (1905), on which Chesterton concentrates in the Wells chapter in *Heretics*, Wells was proposing compulsory sterilization for a second offence of child-bearing by the stupid or improvident, and the isolation of social undesirables (including thieves, the mentally handicapped, and the psychiatrically disturbed) on islands policed in such a way as to keep the sexes apart so as to prevent procreation. For the world population of 1500 million Wells envisages for Utopia, the bureaucracy of the world-state will have on record, in a huge system of buildings in Paris, a number for each individual, accompanied by thumb-print and photograph. As Professor John Carey points out in his incisive study *The Intellectuals and the Masses*, though Wells correctly predicted a number

[130]*The Ball and the Cross*, 320-321.

of modern inventions, the computer technology which would now make this data-tracking project more feasible was not among them.[131] Modestly, Chesterton restricts himself to one comment on the breeding scheme: "medical supervision [may] produce strong and healthy men . . . [but] if it did, the first act of the strong and healthy men would be to smash the medical supervision."[132]

In Chesterton's *The Napoleon of Notting Hill*, which appeared in the same year as *Heretics*, Chesterton satirises the futuristic fantasies of Wells, in which individuals are overshadowed by the technological achievements of science and big government. Adam Wayne takes up his sword against modernizing property developers and defends the dignity of Notting Hill — and thus the liberty that is connected with owning one's own house and garden, however small. As the story unfolds, however, the novel becomes, rather, a critique of the imperialism of Kipling and Rhodes. Notting Hill made the mistake of seeking to impose its powers and way of life on all London. After its defeat by the other boroughs in the battle of Kensington Gardens, Wayne admits this was a merited punishment for corporate egotism. "Notting Hill, having made itself a nation, succumbed to vanity by becoming an empire."[133]

More widely, Chesterton considered that Wells's scientism lands him in a hopeless relativism. Wells's philosophy is a denial of the very possibility of philosophy, since in his hostility to the Platonic concept of truth as timeless, Wells holds there are no secure or reliable ideas on which the intellect can come satisfactorily to rest. His own intellectual journey ended pretty sadly. Ten years after

---

[131] J. Carey, *The Intellectuals and the Masses* , 127-128.

[132] *Heretics*, 43.

[133] J. P. Corrin, G. K. *Chesterton and Hilaire Belloc: The Battle against Modernity*, 4.

G. K. Chesterton, Theologian

Chesterton's death, in *Mind at the End of Its Tether*, Wells concluded it was hopeless to "trace a cosmic pattern of any sort," and impossible to resist the conclusion that "*homo sapiens* is in his present form played out."[134]

Chesterton on the Wider Evolutionism

The way in which Wells had earlier looked to science as the panacea for all human ills was not, of course, a phenomenon restricted to himself. In a pre-Dawkins universe, the turn of the nineteenth and twentieth centuries was the approximate zenith of natural-scientific self-confidence. Even more endemic at that period was belief in the inevitability of evolution towards a higher condition, whether such evolution took, with science, a material or, with Idealist philosophy, a spiritual form. Around 1900 a quite extraordinary publishing success attended the English translation of the German cosmologist Ernst Haeckel's *Welträtsel* as *The Riddle of the Universe.*[135] A work to which Chesterton's early writings

[134]H. G. Wells, *Mind at the End of Its Tether* (London, 1946), 17, 18; cf. M. R. Hillegas, *The Future as Nightmare: H. G. Wells and the Anti-Utopians* (New York, 1967).

[135]E. Haeckel, *Welträtsel* (1900); English translation: *Riddle of the Universe: At the Close of the Nineteenth Century* (London, 1900, 1902). A supplementary volume was published as *Wonder of Life: A Popular Study of Biological Philosophy* (London, 1904). Other translations appeared as *History of Creation* (London, 1892), *The Last Link: Our Present Knowledge of the Descent of Man* (London, 1898), *Evolution of Man* (London, 1905), and *Last Words on Evolution* (London, 1906). For his life see *Biographie in Briefen. Ernst Haeckel* (Gütersloh, 1984). Especially pertinent to Chesterton's critique of Haeckel is the latter's *Monism as Connecting Religion and Science: The Confession of Faith of a Man of Science* (London, 1894). The most recent study is R. J. Richards, *The Tragic Sense of Life: Ernst Haeckel and the Struggle Over Evolutionary Thought* (Chicago, 2008).

make frequent reference, it promised, in Coates's words, "a vast, uniform, uninterrupted and eternal process of development, linking organic and inorganic, matter and spirit, life and art."[136] Haeckel was, as it were, Charles Darwin transfigured by the German traditions of cultural Romanticism and philosophical Idealism.

Coates's claim that Chesterton was struggling with not only materialist but idealist versions of evolutionism turns especially on the figures of Caird and Green. The English Hegelian Edward Caird, Master of Balliol during Belloc's time there, belonged to a school which theoretically was in reaction against philosophical materialism. But a Neo-Idealist Caird still subscribed — so Coates points out — to an evolutionary myth, albeit one whose key concept was not so much matter as the Absolute. For Caird, the universe contained no antagonisms that could not be reconciled by finding their place in a higher unity manifesting itself in a process of organic development. There was neither truth *simpliciter* nor falsehood *simpliciter*, though one could ask how much truth has been expressed with what inadequacies or unexplained assumptions in the ongoing outworking of the dialectic of spirit. In the highly influential writing of Caird's colleague T. H. Green, human knowledge is authenticated to the extent that, starting from an animal condition, we become the vehicle of, or are identified with, an eternally complete consciousness. In Coates's judgment, the Late Victorian commitment to evolutionism of such widely differing kinds shows how Nietzscheanism could be so rapidly assimilated in the Edwardian epoch: that wider phenomenon was likewise Chesterton's broader object of attack. For Chesterton, the idea of a predetermined movement onwards and upwards was an ideologically simplistic substitute for religion, as well as an empirically false supposition.

[136]J. D. Coates, *Chesterton and the Edwardian Cultural Crisis*, 34.

Revolt into Sanity

The last chapters of *Heretics* might be thought somewhat dis-appointing. The book seems to peter out, by spreading its wings too widely to take in a number of distinctly minor figures, or by tackling issues that are merely sectorial rather than total world-views (ethnic identity, the family, aristocracy, the artistic tem-perament, the meaning of the phrase "young nations," or how to write novels about the poor). But what Chesterton is seeking to express is what Gabriel Syme in *The Man Who Was Thursday* calls "revolt against revolt." As we read in that novel: "Being sur-rounded with every conceivable kind of revolt from infancy, Ga-briel had to revolt into something, so he revolted into the only thing left — sanity."[137]

He was certainly provoked. As we hear:

His father cultivated art and self-realisation; his mother went in for simplicity and hygiene. Hence the child, dur-ing his tenderer years, was wholly unacquainted with any drink between the extremes of absinthe and cocoa, of both of which he had a healthy dislike. The more his mother preached a more than Puritan abstinence, the more did his father expand into a more than pagan lati-tude, and by the time the former had come to enforcing vegetarianism, the latter had reached the point of de-fending cannibalism.[138]

So Syme was vulnerable to the blandishments of a philosophical policeman on the Embankment who tells him in the course of re-cruitment to the anti-Anarchist division of the force:

[137]*The Man Who Was Thursday* (1908, 1944), 39.
[138]Ibid., 38-39.

We say that the most dangerous criminal now is the entirely
lawless modern philosopher. Compared to him, burglars and
bigamists are essentially moral men; my heart goes out to
them. They accept the essential ideal of man; they merely
seek it wrongly. Thieves respect property. They merely wish
the property to be their property that they may more perfectly respect it. But philosophers dislike property as property; they wish to destroy the very idea of personal possession.
Bigamists respect marriage, or they would not go through
the highly ceremonial and even ritualistic formality of big-
amy. But philosophers despise marriage as marriage.

To which Syme responds enthusiastically, "The moderns say we
must not punish heretics. My only doubt is whether we have a
right to punish anybody else."[139]

But there is a compensation. In the conclusion of *Heretics*
Chesterton puts it like this:

Truths turn into dogmas the instant they are disputed. Thus
every man who utters a doubt defines a religion. And the
scepticism of our time does not really destroy the beliefs,
rather it creates them; gives them their limits and their
plain and defiant shape . . .

In context, that could and does refer to (political) Liberalism and
patriotism as well as Christianity. So it is when Chesterton spells
out the implications for the latter that Chesterton as theologian
comes to the fore. He writes:

We who are Christians never knew the great philosophic
common sense which inheres in that mystery until the

[139]Ibid., 44.

Anti-Christian writers pointed it out to us. The great march of mental destruction will go on. Everything will become a creed . . . We shall be left defending not only the incredible virtues and sanities of human life, but something more incredible still, this huge impossible universe which stares us in the face. We shall fight for visible prodigies as if they were invisible. We shall look on the impossible grass and the skies with a strange courage. We shall be of those who have seen and yet have believed.[140]

That brings us conveniently to the topic of Chesterton's discovery of metaphysical realism. The sanities he sought to defend, over against fashionable but ultimately lunatic intellectual trends, were all linked to this discovery. The world is a world of things, with their intrinsic properties, and these things and properties (a Scholastic might call them substantial forms) enter the human mind in a commerce wholly native to that mind. Human nature, being one of those things, retains its consistency through all changes of epoch and culture, and its reasonable standards (again, the "perennial philosophy" would term these "natural law") are intrinsic to the flourishing of our kind. Neither things nor standards are self-explanatory. They require grounding, and the name of the ground is "God." These convictions might be counter-cultural for many who inhabited Chesterton's intellectual milieu. That did not make them the less foundational.

---

[140] *Heretics*, 190-191.

Chapter 3

~

The Discovery of Metaphysical Realism

Chesterton was unashamedly a cultural populist, as opposed to a cultural elitist. He was far from minded to agree with those of his intellectual contemporaries who scorned the educational level reached, or even not reached, by the early-twentieth-century "masses." In *Thus Spoke Zarathustra* Nietzsche had declared: "Many too many are born, and they hang on their branches much too long. I wish a storm would come and shake all this rottenness and worm-eatenness from the tree!"[141] For Nietzsche, all fountains are poisoned where the rabble drink.[142] The State, which from the mid-nineteenth century onwards took initiatives in education previously left to private charity or the Church, was, he thought, invented for the masses, or "the superfluous," as his hero-prophet Zarathustra terms them. In the State's monstrous embrace "universal slow suicide is called life."[143] In his *The Will to Power* Nietzsche

[141] F. Nietzsche, *Thus Spoke Zarathustra* (English translation, Harmondsworth, 1961), 75-77. I owe this and the following citations from Nietzsche's writings to J. Carey, *The Intellectuals and the Masses.*

[142] F. Nietzsche, *Thus Spoke Zarathustra*, 98.

[143] Ibid., 120.

called for a "declaration of war on the masses by higher men,"[144] for "everywhere the mediocre are combining in order to make themselves master."[145] John Carey has gone so far as to regard Nietzsche's words as key to the attitude of the European, including the English, intelligentsia in the years 1880 to 1939, or roughly throughout Chesterton's lifetime. Carey's thesis is that:

> modernist literature and art can be seen as a hostile reaction to the unprecedentedly large reading public created by late nineteenth century educational reforms. The purpose of modernist writing . . . was to exclude these newly educated (or "semi-educated") readers, and so to preserve the intellectual's seclusion from the "mass."[146]

In sharp contrast, Chesterton's adoption of a career as a journalist signalled a willingness on his part to throw himself with gusto into the reading world of the newly educated public. His trust in common humanity overbore all other considerations.

This is not to suggest, however, that Chesterton regarded the print media of his day with total indulgence. They at any rate *were* able to poison wells, especially where people had become detached from traditional culture. At the time of Christ's Passion the Jerusalem populace had swung over to support a baseless assertion — the moral superiority of Barabbas over Jesus. In *The Everlasting Man* Chesterton compares this with the city populations of his own day, over-influenced by "newspaper scares and scoops."[147] Chesterton

---

[144]F. Nietzsche, *The Will to Power* (English translation, London, 1968), 77.

[145]Ibid., 382.

[146]J. Carey, *The Intellectuals and the Masses*, vii.

[147]*The Everlasting Man* ([1925] San Francisco, 1993), 211.

was especially worried by the way popularised versions of sceptical or hyper-sophisticated philosophies were circulating. That is relevant to the issue of metaphysical realism, a philosophy which, over against all forms of reductionist empiricism and solipsistic Idealism, he saw as native to the human mind and, moreover, a condition of that mind's sanity and flourishing. As he put it in his study of Cobbett, "This great delusion of the prior claim of printed matter, as something anterior to experience and capable of contradicting it, is the main weakness of modern urban society."[148] In this regard, the authority of print was not necessarily on the side of the angels.

Chesterton's discovery of metaphysical realism, a discovery later refined by the — rather cavalier — reading which went into his *Saint Thomas Aquinas* (his genius meant he had little need to burn the midnight oil), was meant to be a vindication of the experience of the common man. But metaphysical realism is not merely the upshot of a commonsense epistemology. As practised within the Christian tradition (and the Jewish and Islamic traditions likewise, for that matter) metaphysical realism is also a fruit of the doctrine of creation, which declares things to be intelligibly planned by the divine mind who called them "good."

> The primordial things — existence, energy, fruition — are good so far as they go . . . The ordinary modern progressive position is that this is a bad universe, but will certainly get better. I say it is a good universe, even if it gets worse.[149]

So the metaphysical realism Chesterton discovered combines these two: commonsense epistemology and the doctrine of creation.

[148]*William Cobbett*, 145.

[149]*The Apostle and the Wild Ducks, and Other Essays*, ed. D. Collins (London, 1975), 164, 165.

We have already investigated Chesterton's attitude towards the secular "heresies" of Shaw, Wells, Kipling, and Rhodes, as well as his reaction to the wider group of monistic evolutionists — both materialist and Idealist — of Chesterton's youth and early manhood. We now turn our attention to *Orthodoxy*, Chesterton's response to the secular "heresies" of the Edwardian era, in which he takes on what he calls the "mad doctors" who "occupy half the chairs of science and seats of learning."[150]

Intellectual Lunacy

In selecting the word "mad" to describe the professors and scientists of his day, Chesterton is not simply choosing any insulting term that comes to hand. As *Orthodoxy* opens, he is found arguing that it is characteristic of maniacs that their minds move in a perfect but narrow circle. Within their own limited terms of reference, lunatics are often cogently rational. As he writes, "The lunatic's theory explains a large number of things, but it does not explain them in a large way."[151] Chesterton takes the mark of madness to be the "combination between a logical completeness and a spiritual contraction."[152] Madmen are "in the clean and well-lit prison of one idea . . ."[153] The situation is likewise with contemporary intellectuals: these thinkers exhibit "the combination of an expansive and exhaustive reason with a contracted common sense."[154] Thus, in the materialism of Ernst Haeckel (several of whose books had been translated by Joseph McCabe, one of the minor rationalists

---

[150]*Orthodoxy* (London, 1908, 1996), 22.

[151]Ibid., 18.

[152]Ibid.

[153]Ibid., 21.

[154]Ibid., 22.

to whom Chesterton devoted a chapter of *Heretics*), cosmic order is to be explained by a matter-based determinism. Chesterton sums up the world-view of Haeckel's *The Riddle of the Universe* in these words: "all things, even the souls of men, are leaves inevitably unfolding on an utterly unconscious tree."[155] The explanation, comments Chesterton, does explain, but at the price of leaving us with the feeling that, if this is the real cosmos, it is not much of one. On this account: "the whole of life is something much more grey, narrow and trivial than many separate aspects of it" (Chesterton has already named, for instance, fighting peoples, proud mothers, first love, fear on the seas, and he will go on to add kindness, hope, courage, poetry, initiative, and, in a portmanteau phrase, everything distinctively human). And so, "The parts seem greater than the whole."[156]

By contrast, metaphysical realism, as an account of cosmic order hospitable to the Christian doctrine of creation, can improve on the materialist account: whereas Christians are free to believe that there are large areas of "settled order and inevitable development" in the universe, materialists, Chesterton points out, cannot allow the slightest incursion of spirit or miracle.[157] Chesterton returns to the topic of Haeckel's materialist monism on numerous occasions, right up until the end of his life, rightly discerning that this kind of thinking would be a major contender for the allegiance of intellectuals for a long time to come. In *The Well and the Shadows*, published the year before his death, he speaks of Haeckel's materialism lying on science "like a dead hand," mentioning how the prospect of conceivably forwarding Haeckelianism almost deterred

[155] Ibid., 23-24.
[156] Ibid., 24.
[157] Ibid., 25.

Darwin from publishing *The Descent of Man*, according to Darwin's own account in the introduction to that work.[158] Chesterton saw Haeckelianism as a monstrously inflated version of Darwinism, for Haeckel had turned evolution into what the historian of science Stanley Jaki has termed a "mimicry of the Creed," with its own trinity of divinities which Jaki defines as: the inchoateness of the universe; the spontaneous origin of life, and the automatic rise of human consciousness.[159]

After materialism, a second philosophical error is solipsism, a kind of "logical completeness" married to "spiritual contraction." In general, Chesterton saw solipsism more existentially than theoretically. He considered it chiefly a pathological state of mind, indeed, "the real and ever threatening alternative to normal existence."[160] In this perspective, Kantian philosophy and post-Kantian philosophies of the transcendental ego, according to which our grasp of the sensuous forms of reality depends on the origination of forms of thought from the "I," are dangerous sirens, luring the unwary onto the solipsistic rocks. In his *Autobiography* he noted: "At a very early age I had thought my way back to thought itself. It was a very dreadful thing to do; for it may lead to thinking that there is nothing but thought."[161] Chesterton's principal literary exploration of solipsism would take the form of his 1929 novel of ideas, *The Poet and the Lunatics*. There the hero, Gabriel Gale, is both populist and sane, whereas the elitists are egoists who go mad by making themselves the centre of their world. Being a poet is the correct profession for Gale, since, so Chesterton writes,

[158]*The Well and the Shadows* (London, 1935), 56.

[159]S. L. Jaki, *Chesterton: A Seer of Science* (Urbana, Illinois, 1986), 63.

[160]Ibid., 87.

[161]*Autobiography*, 92.

the artist's role is to be "centric . . . [Genius] . . . ought to be in the core of the cosmos, not on the revolving edges."[162] Already in *Orthodoxy* Chesterton understands solipsism as what he terms "panegoism." The moral as well as ontological connotations of the word "egoism" enable Chesterton to make the term "solipsism" stretch so as to include writers who, as Chesterton puts it, try to "impress their own personalities" rather than, by their use of the literary imagination, create life for the world. Into the same category fall those Nietzscheans seeking the Superman who are always "looking for him in the looking-glass."[163] In each case there is an inability to believe one lives outside an all-consuming dream of self.

More widely, the two great errors — materialism, solipsism — have something in common. As Chesterton puts it in *Orthodoxy*:

> The man who cannot believe his senses [the solipsist] and the man who cannot believe anything else [the materialist] are both insane, but their insanity is proved not by any error in their argument, but by the manifest mistake of their whole lives.[164]

Locked up in twin boxes, they cannot get out into health and happiness, whether that be, as in the case of the materialist, the wider realm of heaven, or, as in that of the solipsist, the wider realm of earth.[165] Chesterton admits that in this critique he is bringing to bear a pragmatic criterion, but he accompanies it

---

[162]*The Poet and the Lunatics*, 24-25.

[163]*Orthodoxy*, 28.

[164]Ibid., 29.

[165]See on this A. D. Nuttal, *The Common Sky: Philosophy and the Literary Imagination* (Berkeley, California, 1974).

with a theoretical one. What these two errors have in common is they use reason "in a void," without awareness of the "proper first principles" by reference to which the exercise of reason should proceed.[166]

Just as in *Heretics*, then, Chesterton recovered the faith of the Church about man by a process of contestation of contemporary ideologies, so in *Orthodoxy* Chesterton wants us to infer what those "proper first principles" are by means of the challenge he issues to improper first principles, as found in various false philosophical, and especially epistemological, starting-points.

We recall how in *Heretics* Chesterton was sometimes worried by particular erroneous principles which individual thinkers had espoused, but sometimes also by a refusal to declare a cosmic philosophy at all. This second phenomenon, the withdrawal from intellectual commitment — which occurs most notably in the opening sections of the book, and which Coates thinks reflects the early years of Edward VII's reign — still preoccupies him in *Orthodoxy*. It is not now, however, as in *Heretics*, an essay on culture, simply a false if fashionable humility about making wide-ranging truth-claims. It is in *Orthodoxy*, an essay on epistemology and metaphysics, something more worrying: an outright scepticism about the value of "the instrument" — namely, the human mind. Why should not good logic be as misleading as bad logic, if both are "movements in the brain of a bewildered ape"?[167] In the wrong hands, Darwinian thought can secrete this ruinous corrosive. As Chesterton writes: "Evolution is either an innocent scientific description of how certain

[166] *Orthodoxy*, 30.
[167] Ibid., 39.

earthly things came about; or, if it is anything more than this, it is an attack on thought itself."[168]

The preceding discussion does not exhaust Chesterton's inventory of varieties of intellectual madness. His range as a philosophical interlocutor of his own contemporaries is demonstrated in taking further the criticisms he had offered of them in *Heretics*. Other examples of epistemological errors spotted by Chesterton include: Wells's nominalism, for which all separate things are unique and there are no classes of object, to which Chesterton replies, "Thinking means connecting things, and stops if they cannot be connected,"[169] and the relativistic version of the doctrine of progress, for which standards are constantly changing. As Chesterton asks, "If the standard changes, how can there be improvement, which implies a standard?"[170] Chesterton had already noted that particular weakness in *Heretics*.

Chesterton agrees that there is an imperative need to accept the "things that are necessary to the human mind," [171] and he is willing to use a pragmatist argument as what he calls a "preliminary guide to truth." Yet he recognizes that a systematic pragmatism would be self-defeating as a form of reason. As Chesterton puts it, "One of those necessities [of the human mind] is a belief in objective truth."[172]

Chesterton has a clear overall response to these mistaken intellectual gambits. If things can be questioned wildly — that is, without respect for metaphysical realism, or an account of things

---

[168]Ibid., 41.
[169]Ibid., 42.
[170]Ibid., 43.
[171]Ibid., 44.
[172]Ibid., 44-45.

as interrelated in a cosmic ordering, with *homo sapiens*, cognitively equipped to grasp the intelligibility of things, specially placed among them — then the rational life will not long survive. At the present time, writes Chesterton, "we can hear scepticism crashing through the old ring of authorities, and at the same moment we can see reason swaying upon her throne."[173] There must be on our part a fiduciary consent to the claim that human thinking is reality-related, that human knowing really grasps the intelligibility of the real and can proceed to express it in words. Otherwise, reason will not be able to sustain — indeed, even to begin — its work. This is what Chesterton means by saying, "It is idle to talk always of the alternative of reason and faith. Reason is itself a matter of faith."[174] Naturally, by "faith" here Chesterton doesn't mean specifically Christian faith. He is speaking of a philosophical faith grounding confidence in the fundamental reliability of the human mind and its most refined instrument, which is language. Here Chesterton may be placed in a long line of English public moralists going back to Newman and Coleridge.[175]

The Limits of Necessitarianism

Before looking at what Chesterton made of one particularly profound and venerable version of a rationally functioning metaphysical realism, namely, that of Aquinas, we should notice the distinctive spin he puts on such realism in *Orthodoxy*. Chesterton distinguishes sharply between, on the one hand, what he calls "the science of mental relations" in which, as he remarks, "there

---

[173]*Orthodoxy*, 40.

[174]Ibid., 39.

[175] See, for example, J. Coulson, *Newman and the Common Tradition* (Oxford, 1970).

really are laws" (necessary entailments as in mathematical and logical reasoning), and, on the other hand, the "science of physical facts" in which, he writes, "there are no laws but only weird repetitions."[176] Chesterton is rightly suspicious of the concept of laws of nature, if the word "law" is to be construed as necessitating in a strict sense. As Stanley Jaki has put it: "Chesterton's stunning insistence . . . that science as such gives only logical identities and relations but no realities, should make him appear an interpreter of science to be ranked with a Duhem and a Meyerson. . . ."[177] The latter two figures mentioned were early-twentieth-century practising scientists who were also notable philosophers of science. Jaki explains that Pierre Duhem (1861-1916) "asserted the primacy of objective reality, to which common sense and not the exertions of logic, science or not, gave the only access,"[178] while Emile Meyerson (1859-1933) spelt out, if in a "muted and at times roundabout way" the "inference that if only the identity relations of mathematical physics existed, nothing in reality would ever *happen*."[179] Whereas Darwin's disciple and philosophical populariser Thomas Huxley considered that counting ordinary sequences of events furnished a sufficient argument for positing unalterable cosmic law, for Chesterton no such conclusiveness attached to the act of inference involved. Where the repetition of cosmic sequence is concerned, we do not so much count on it as bet on it.

[176]*Orthodoxy*, 67-68.

[177]S. L. Jaki, *Chesterton, A Seer of Science*, 26.

[178]Ibid., p. 23. Duhem's *Théorie physique* (Paris, 1906) is further explored in Jaki's study, *Uneasy Genius: The Life and Work of Pierre Duhem* (Dordrecht, 1984); Meyerson's treatise *Identité et réalité* is dated to the following year, 1907.

[179]S. L. Jaki, *Chesterton, A Seer of Science*, op. cit., 26.

When we are considering the actual existence of things, the inappropriateness of necessitarianism is only matched for Chesterton by the appropriateness of an enduring attitude of wonder or surprise. As Chesterton puts it in expounding the "ethics of elfland." "The repetition in nature may not be a mere recurrence; it may be a theatrical *encore*."[180] Owing to their abounding vitality, children can go on doing the same thing, or wanting an adult to do it, times beyond number. By analogy, the Author of nature, who must be boundlessly more vital than they, may "exult in monotony," so that repetition may continue for millennia by mere choice and then suddenly stop. To account for real existence, *will* is a far more useful concept than law. In their non-necessity, facts are miracles in a broad sense of the word by the way they arouse or should arouse wonder: marvelling. Here is where Chesterton locates the strictly rational need for imagination. In his first book of essays, the 1901 collection *The Defendant*, he had described the function of imagination as "not so much to make strange things settled as to make settled things strange, not so much to make wonders facts as to make facts wonders."[181] Chesterton asks in this context whether by being ultimately "wilful" facts may not also be called miracles in the strict sense as well.

The Model of the Artwork in Cosmic Philosophy

In so asking, he raises the further question: Is there purpose, and therefore personality, behind the world? Chesterton compares the limited order which characterises the world to that of a work of art, whose existence one would hardly register without positing in some way that of the artist. As he would write in *Saint Thomas*

---

[180]*Orthodoxy*, 82.

[181]*The Defendant* (London, 1901), 84.

Aquinas, the question of a transcendental creative matrix for the world is unavoidable.

> For those who really think, there is always something really unthinkable about the evolutionary cosmos, as they [integral Evolutionists à la Haeckel] conceive it; because it is something coming out of nothing; an ever-increasing flood of water pouring out of an empty jug. In a word, the world does not explain itself, and cannot do so merely by continuing to expand itself.[182]

According to Chesterton, the root concept of Christian theism was that "God was a creator, as an artist is a creator."[183]

> A poet is so separate from his poem that he himself speaks of it as a little thing he has "thrown off." Even in giving it forth he has flung it away. The principle that all creation and procreation is a breaking-off is at least as consistent through the cosmos as the evolutionary principle that all growth is a branching out. A woman loses a child even in having a child. All creation is separation.[184]

And Chesterton calls it the "prime philosophical principle of Christianity" that this "divorce in the divine act of making" is the "true description of the act whereby the divine energy made the world."[185]

He considers two main objections. According to the first, the sheer scale of the cosmos makes the comparison with an artwork

---

[182]*Saint Thomas Aquinas* (London, 1933), 215-216.

[183]*Orthodoxy*, 10.

[184]Ibid., 111.

[185]Ibid.

limp. Chesterton disputes the claim that the cosmos is "large" in scale, on the ground that, since there is only one of them, comparison is senseless. If someone wishes to say, "I like this vast cosmos, with its throng of stars and its crowd of varied creatures," he may do so, but he cannot dispute the right of another to say, "I like this cosy little cosmos, with its decent number of stars and as neat a provision of livestock as I wish to see."[186] And indeed, Chesterton considers that the "dim dogmas of vitality" expressed in the notion of a personally purposive artefact are better served by calling the world small rather than large. He reports a

> fierce and pious care which I felt touching the pricelessness and the peril of life . . . I felt about the golden sun and the silver moon as a schoolboy feels if he has one sovereign and one shilling.[187]

Chesterton would surely have been struck by more recent astrophysical investigation of the early phases of the history of the universe, where, as one traces time backwards, it shrinks to the dimension of a star, a planet, and from there in microseconds to the size of a pinhead. As Jaki (again) writes, it seems a demand of reason to accept that such a cosmos is "radically contingent on a supracosmic choice for its existence."[188]

At this same foundational level of response to the world, Chesterton waves away a second objection — the problem of evil which, since late antiquity, has been a major difficulty in the idea of the issue of the world from a non-maleficent Creator. Chesterton

---

[186] *Orthodoxy*, 86.

[187] Ibid., 87.

[188] S. L. Jaki, *Chesterton, A Seer of Science*, 112.

replies that moral reactions along the spectrum, "cosmos good, cosmos bad," are irrelevant here. As he remarks:

> The assumption of it is that a man criticises this world as if he were house-hunting, as if he were being shown over a new suite of apartments. If a man came to this world from some other world in full possession of his powers he might discuss whether the advantage of mid-summer woods made up for the disadvantage of mad dogs, just a man looking for lodgings might balance the presence of a telephone against the absence of a sea-view. But no man is in this position . . . My acceptance of the universe is not optimism, it is more like patriotism. It is a matter of primary loyalty.[189]

Pessimism or Optimism?

After his Slade School experiences, Chesterton was never tempted again by pessimism. That life is a gift immensely valuable and immensely valued may be proved, he wrote in *The Thing*, by the simple device of "putting a pistol to the head of a pessimist."[190] In his novel *Man Alive*, a Cambridge undergraduate, Innocent Smith, gives a Schopenhauerian (and therefore a pessimist), the Warden of Brakespeare College, whom he has driven out of his rooms onto an adjacent Gothic buttress, the options of either having his brains blown out or repeating after him the lines: "I thank the goodness and the grace/ That on my birth have smiled/ And perched me on this curious place,/ A happy English child," which in these particular circumstances Dr Eames is only too glad to do.[191]

---

[189] *Orthodoxy*, 92, 93.

[190] *The Thing* (London, 1929), 62.

[191] *Manalive* (London, 1912, 1921), 165.

G. K. Chesterton, Theologian

In sharp contrast to his denial in *Orthodoxy* of any imputation of optimism, in his study of the artist George Frederick Watts Chesterton had accepted the self-description "optimist" in a cosmic context. It would, however, be incorrect to suppose he had changed his mind, for in the Watts book he had given the word a sense all his own. He writes:

> One optimism [the variety he repudiates] says that this is the best of all possible worlds. The other says that it is certainly not the best of all possible worlds, but it is the best of all possible things that a world should be possible.[192]

For the cosmic patriot, such as Chesterton considered himself to be:

> The world is not a lodging-house at Brighton, which we are to leave because it is miserable. It is the fortress of our family, with the flag flying on the turret, and the more miserable it is, the less we should leave it.[193]

What is wrong with the pessimist is not that he "chastises gods and men" but that he "does not love what he chastises."[194] He fails in primary loyalty to things. Should he put this failure right, the problem of evil would take on its correct proportions, which are not those of a theoretical difficulty about divine origination but those of a practical challenge to human ameliorative effort.

Here Chesterton's cameo portrait of Lord Byron in his 1902 study *Twelve Types* is instructive. Byron, writes Chesterton, was to all appearances an uncompromising conscious pessimist. But a moral challenge, the "cold, hard political necessity" to help the

[192] *G. F. Watts*, 66-67.
[193] *Orthodoxy*, 93.
[194] Ibid., 97.

Greeks in their bid for freedom from their Turkish oppressors, revealed an unconscious optimist beneath — even though Byron's participation in the Greek War of Independence was medically disastrous for him and brought him to his death.

> In Greece [Byron] heard the cry of reality, and all the time that he was dying, he began to live. He heard suddenly the call of that buried and subconscious happiness which is in all of us, and which may emerge suddenly at the sight of the grass of a meadow, or the spears of the enemy.[195]

The Significance of Freedom

The reference to human freedom here is important. As Chesterton explains in *Orthodoxy*, in making the world, God precisely set it free. Christian doctrine can help out philosophy here by reference to the idea of theological dramatics. Chesterton anticipates the Swiss dogmatician Hans Urs von Balthasar's notion of "theo-drama": the interaction of freedoms, human and divine. As he writes:

> God had written, not so much a poem, but rather a play; a play he had planned as perfect, but which had necessarily been left to human actors and stage-managers, who had since made a great mess of it.[196]

That raises the question of how Chesterton saw ethics in a theological perspective, an issue which I shall be considering in chapter 8; meanwhile we can note that the defence of free will is

---

[195]*Twelve Types*, 44.

[196]*Orthodoxy*, 111. That is the theme of Chesterton's last play, *The Surprise*.

central to Chesterton's metaphysical realism inasmuch as the latter includes the recognition of human will as genuine albeit conditioned choice. Part of metaphysical realism is to accept the testimony not only of the senses in relation to the shared external world but also of common human self-report with regard to the internal world constantly exposed externally in moral action. If Chesterton disliked an inflated evolutionism for abolishing forms in favour of flux, his strongest opposition was reserved for its attempt to elide that deepest sort of ontological form which is the immortal human soul (the "form of the body"), with its native capacity for freedom. Mechanistic ontologies pre-empt that freedom, whereas metaphysical realism warrants it, not least by generating an account of reality as issuing from divine will. A world brought into existence by free divine will is a place congruent with the exercise of free human will.[197] In the 1912 novel *Manalive* the "wind" which blows Innocent Smith over the garden-wall of a suburban boarding-house so as to rejuvenate the attitudes of the young people staying there is clearly meant to be the Holy Spirit, who, in the teaching of Jesus, "lists where he will" (John 3:8). As the narrator explains, this is the "good wind that blows nobody harm."[198]

Chesterton's Discovery of Thomism

Chesterton's decision to compose an account of Thomas and Thomism as a complement to his study of Francis of Assisi and Franciscanism obliged him to take further the discovery of metaphysical realism. In an introductory note, Chesterton explains he has taken the view that a biography of Thomas will be an

---

[197]Cf. S. L. Jaki, *Chesterton, A Seer of Science*, 20.
[198]*Manalive*, 10.

introduction to his philosophy, just as Thomas's philosophy is an introduction to his theology. Chesterton confesses that he can only take the reader "just beyond the first stage of the story": in other words, to broach the theology but not cover it. Aquinas appealed to him as a resource for resolving the crisis in the philosophical order which affected Chesterton's intellectual environment as he had come to view it in *Heretics* if not before. Actually, Chesterton was convinced of metaphysical realism well before the religious development of his thought took off on its distinctive trajectory. Some years prior to his adoption of a doctrinally based Christianity he concluded that "where there is anything there is God," and sensed an organic link between the real and its source in divine creativity.[199] For a Thomist the explanation of both affirmations would be divine presence in all things by way of creative causality. It was the complete congruence of Thomas's philosophical-theological outlook with Chesterton's pre-existing commitment to a theistically ordered realism, amplified in its dogmatically reworked articulation in *Orthodoxy*, that explains Chesterton's attraction to Thomism. To this may be added as a subsidiary factor, after his conversion to Catholicism in the pontificate of Pius XI and hence wider exposure to Aquinas (this was the high point of the Thomist revival and official magisterial approval for Thomism in the Church of Rome), his conviction that, as he put it:

> It is a paradox of history that each generation is converted by the saint who contradicts it most, and as St Francis appealed to the prosaic nineteenth century, so St Thomas has a special message for our own irrational generation . . .

[199]See "A Crazy Tale," cited in M. Ward, *Gilbert Keith Chesterton*, 19, and *Autobiography*, 150-151.

— the generation, namely, by this juncture, of the 1930s. Adam Schwartz calls Chesterton's Aquinas book "a non-fictional allegory of Chesterton's own era, as he felt that Thomas's mediaeval foes had re-emerged in modernity."[200]

What points does Chesterton highlight from Thomas's corpus? They are underlinings of Chestertonian insights already achieved, and so will not surprise us. Here we can mention five in particular, of which the initial two may be indicated quite briefly.

In the first place, Thomas is manifestly committed to the notion that body and mind belong equally to the human person so that, as Chesterton writes, claiming for further justification D. H. Lawrence as well as Walt Whitman, "[The human being] can only be a balance and union" of the two.[201] Secondly, Chesterton insists on Thomas's presentation of freedom, which Aquinas had linked, via St John Damascene, to the biblical doctrine of man's imagehood of God.

Thirdly, and this is the first of three points that require slightly more explanation, Chesterton correctly reports that (owing, in fact, to Aquinas's account of secondary causality), Thomas "stands for . . . subordinate sovereignties or autonomies." He was "always defending the independence of dependent things."[202] He notes Thomas's inhospitality to monism: for Aquinas, he observes, pigs are pigs, not epiphenomena of an underlying One. In *Christendom in Dublin*, written in 1932, the year before *Saint Thomas Aquinas*, Chesterton stated his belief that such an anti-monistic pluralism is a precondition of poetry.

Pantheism has been attributed to the poets, but in truth Pantheism is the very opposite of poetry. Poetry is that

[200] A. Schwartz, *The Third Spring*, 101.
[201] *Saint Thomas Aquinas*, 27.
[202] Ibid., 29.

separation of the soul from some object, whereby we can re-gard it with wonder, whereas Pantheism turns all things into one thing, which cannot wonder at itself.[203]

Chesterton sees that while such a doctrine of natural kinds is common sense, it is not, for Thomas, mere common sense, but is connected with the dogma of creation, or as Chesterton writes: "a Creator who created pigs, as distinct from a Cosmos that merely evolved them."[204] That will be connected to the fifth and final of my "underlinings." Meanwhile we can note how Chesterton con-fessed in the *Autobiography* that "all my life I have loved edges; and the boundary-line that brings one thing sharply against another. All my life I have loved frames and limits."[205]

In the fourth place, Chesterton stresses that, for Thomas, these points of anthropology and cosmology belong with a dis-tinctive overall scheme whose cardinal teaching is a theological, rather than naturalistic, materialism with its climax in Chris-tology. This is not entirely a *novum* for Chesterton, except in the clarity and force with which it is now expressed. He says: "As compared with a Jew, a Moslem, a Buddhist, a Deist, or most ob-vious alternatives, a Christian *means* a man who believes that deity or sanctity has attached to matter or entered the world of

---

[203] *Christendom in Dublin*, 33-34. Or, as he wrote the following year: "That *strangeness* of things which is the light in all poetry, and in-deed in all art, is really connected with their otherness, or what is called their objectivity," *Saint Thomas Aquinas*, 147. This was Chesterton's long-standing conviction. In his Blake book he had written of mediaeval illuminations: "The Christian decorators, being true mystics, were chiefly concerned to maintain the real-ity of objects. For the highest dogma of the spiritual is to affirm the material," *William Blake*, 135.

[204] *Saint Thomas Aquinas*, 30.

[205] *Autobiography*, 25.

the senses."[206] Whereas the Crusaders wanted to recover the places where Christ's body had been, because they held them to be, consequently, Christian places, the "holy places": "St Thomas wanted to recover what was in essence the body of Christ itself; the sanctified body of the Son of Man which had become a miraculous medium between heaven and earth."[207] In rather more technical terms, the crucified and glorified embodied humanity of the Word incarnate continues to be the instrumental cause of humankind's salvation.

Fifthly and lastly, Thomism for Chesterton combines common-sense evaluation of reality with the doctrine of creation. So on the one hand, we can find Chesterton writing as follows: "The motto of the Mystics has always been, 'Taste and see.' Now St Thomas also began by saying, 'Taste and see,' but he said it of the first rudimentary impressions of the human animal."[208] That is common sense, or in the often-repeated Thomist maxim, "Everything that is in the intellect has been in the senses."[209] But on the other hand, Chesterton does not simply make Thomas into a second Dr Johnson, who proves the existence of a stone by kicking it. Instead, Chesterton follows the movement of Thomas's own thought as it finds in the finite being presented through the senses a way to the fontal being which pours itself out in all that is. He thus highlights the doctrine of creation too. Chesterton speaks of the "*positive* position of [Thomas's] mind, which is filled and soaked as with sunshine, with the warmth of the wonder of created things," in such a way that just as Carmelite nuns take "titles of devotion"

---

[206] *Saint Thomas Aquinas*, 31.

[207] Ibid.

[208] Ibid., 57.

[209] Cited in *Saint Thomas Aquinas*, 129.

such as "of the Holy Ghost" or "of the Cross," Aquinas could be given, so Chesterton thought, the title "of the Creator."[210] This was a proposal cited by Pope Benedict XVI when, as Cardinal Ratzinger, he preached a homily in honour of St Thomas on 28 January 1987 at the Pontifical University of St Thomas (the Angelicum) in Rome.[211] Chesterton does not omit the corollary, which is that the capacity of the mind to apprehend the creature/Creator relation is an index of its aptitude for a knowledge of God as the First Truth. Returning to his contrast between Thomas's realist epistemology and mystical knowledge, we find Chesterton remarking:

> It might be said that the Thomist begins with something like the taste of an apple, and afterwards deduces a divine life for the intellect; while the Mystic exhausts intellect first, and says finally that the sense of God is something like the taste of an apple.[212]

By which he means I suppose (not being a mystic myself), sweet, crisp, and refreshing. For Thomas God's grace can be, up to a point, perceived, since "he who receives it knows by an experience of sweetness which is not experienced by him who does not receive it."[213]

"Nothing but Yourself"

As is fairly well known, Thomas's thought follows two paths: a "way of ascent," through analogy, from finite things to God, using

---

[210]Ibid., 95.

[211]J. Ratzinger, " 'Consecrate them in the truth': a homily for St Thomas' Day," *New Blackfriars* 68.803 (1987): 112-115.

[212]*Saint Thomas Aquinas*, 57-58.

[213]Thomas Aquinas, *Summa Theologiae* Ia. IIae., Q. 112, art. 5.

the tools of *metaphysics*; and a "way of descent," reproducing the divine self-disclosure in finite materials, using the resources supplied by *revelation*. The normal presentation of the "way of descent" in Thomas's corpus is via the disciplined exploration of Holy Scripture for which the primordially given divine Name is "I AM WHO AM" (Exodus 3:14), a ratification by divine authority of the naming of God as subsistent Being itself in the way of ascent in metaphysics.

Chesterton has warned us, however, that he will not be going beyond the philosophy into the theology. Nevertheless, he signals his awareness that Thomas's theology is not only "anabatic," upward-travelling, but is also "catabatic," downward-travelling, in his interpretation of a celebrated episode in Thomas's biography. That was when in the last year of his life, in December 1273, the saint had a striking visionary — or more strictly, auditory — experience in the priory church of the Dominicans in Naples. According to the biographers, he heard a voice speaking from the great crucifix in that church, San Domenico Maggiore. The voice told him he had spoken well of the Lord, and might name his recompense, to which Thomas replied, *Nihil nisi Te*: "Nothing but Yourself." Chesterton's interpretation of the contemporary accounts stresses how the sheer avidity of Thomas's metaphysically realist thirst for things heightens strikingly the significance of this reply. Thomas, says Chesterton:

> might have asked for any one of a thousand things that would really have satisfied his broad and virile appetite for the very vastness and variety of the universe. The point is that for him, when the voice spoke from beneath the outstretched arms of the Crucified, those arms were truly opened wide, and opening most gloriously the gates of all

the worlds; they were arms pointing to the east and to the west, to the ends of the earth and the very extremes of existence. They were truly spread out with a gesture of omnipotent generosity; the Creator himself offering Creation itself; with all its millionfold mystery of separate beings, and the triumphal chorus of the creatures. That is the blazing background of multitudinous Being that gives the particular strength, and even a sort of surprise, to the answer of St Thomas . . . "I will have Thyself."[214]

---

[214] *Saint Thomas Aquinas*, 108. Chesterton's conviction that Thomism is "the philosophy of common sense," and so, as he puts it, "nearer than most philosophies to the mind of the man in the street" (ibid., 116, 117) does not, then, exhaust his account of Aquinas. Still, the philosophy of common sense matters to him. One can see why the doyen of historians of mediaeval philosophy Étienne Gilson so strongly approved of Chesterton's short and, after all, amateur work, when we find Chesterton anticipating Gilson's own quarrel with Jacques Maritain over the admissibility or otherwise of qualifying the term "critical" in Thomas's case (Gilson thought definitely not). Chesterton notes that it may seem surprising that Thomas "does not deal with what many now think the main metaphysical question: whether we can prove that the primary act of recognition of any reality is real. The answer is that St Thomas recognised instantly what so many modern sceptics have begun to suspect rather laboriously, that a man must either answer that question in the affirmative, or else never answer any question; never ask any question; never even exist intellectually, to answer or to ask" (ibid., 119).

We can notice that Chesterton gives a beautiful little account, in no way misleading, of Thomas on that "act of recognition": ibid., 148-149. The mind is neither merely receptive nor merely creative: "the essence of the Thomist common sense is that two agencies are at work: reality and the recognition of reality; and their meeting is a sort of marriage."

G. K. Chesterton, Theologian

Excursus on the Visionary Dimension
of Chesterton's Metaphysics

It would be a mistake to think that the elevated common sense of Thomist ontology constituted the whole of Chesterton's metaphysical outlook. True, the Thomist ontology had a depth and beauty not apparent in either its Platonist or its Aristotelean forerunners, and that owing to its distinctive foundation in a creation metaphysic indebted to Holy Scripture. But even so, taken by itself, it does not suffice to account for Chesterton's entire vision of the world. His is not only the metaphysical realism of a mainstream twentieth-century Thomist philosopher such as Étienne Gilson. It is also a visionary metaphysics which, like that of one of Thomas's ancient sources, the Pseudo-Denys, acknowledges in symbol an equally far-reaching way of displaying what is involved in the real.

We can see this at once from his early studies of two visual artists, G. F. Watts and William Blake, where Chesterton considers in one case the natural symbolic value of a painting, in the other a poet-illustrator's prolongation of a supernatural symbol from the Scriptures. Chesterton's book on Watts came out in the year of the artist's death, 1904, when Watts, whose mature work consisted in part of portraits, in part of ambitious allegorical paintings, was already falling from favour. Chesterton is chiefly interested in the allegories, and in his account of them presents Watts as a great preacher who sought to speak universally by eschewing any use of signs that are, as Chesterton explains, "local or temporary or topical, even if the locality be a whole continent, the time a stretch of centuries, or the topic a vast civilisation or an undying church . . ."[215] In Watts's symbolic repertoire, we read: "There is

[215]*G. F. Watts*, 34.

nothing here but the eternal things, clay and fire and the sea, and motherhood and the dead."[216]

Though Chesterton appears to be in two minds about the wisdom of this proceeding, an actual encounter with the canvas of Watts's *Mammon* convinces him of the metaphysical reach of painting inspired by this aesthetic. Watts had portrayed Mammon, or the spirit of commerce, as an impressively enthroned man whose face seems, however, blind and somewhat bestial: his ears in particular look asinine. His heavy hand and feet have fallen, "as if [writes Chesterton] by a mere pulverizing accident," on the godlike figures of a young man and young woman beneath him. The background is smoky, as though, to cite Chesterton again, "from some invisible and horrible sacrifice."[217] The common objection by critics is that the painting is a mere literary allegory. Watts could have saved his time by simply putting into words his dislike of commercial exploitation. Chesterton responds:

> It is not true that this is a picture of Commerce; but that Commerce and Watts' picture spring from the same source. There does exist a certain dark and driving force in the world; one of its products is this picture, another is Commerce.[218]

The common positions of allegory and reality, explains Chesterton, are here reversed.

> The fact is not that here we have an effective presentation under a certain symbol of red robes and smoke and a throne, of what the financial world is, but rather that here we have something of the truth that is hidden behind the symbol of

[216]Ibid., 33.
[217]Ibid., 51.
[218]Ibid., 53.

white waistcoats and hats on the back of the head, of financial papers and sporting prophets, of butter closing quiet and Pendragon being meant to win. This is not a symbol of commerce: commerce is a symbol of this.[219]

So Watts "is not a man copying literature or philosophy, but rather a man copying the great spiritual and central realities which literature and philosophy also set out to copy."[220] At the time of writing G. F. Watts, Chesterton was content to explain the correspondence between art and moral truth or moral beauty in purely psychological terms. There is — claims Chesterton in what he calls a "not very extravagant hypothesis" — a "kinship between pictorial and moral harmonies in the psychology of men."[221] Watts's use of colour and line serves such harmony. Chesterton's description of his own aesthetic in this book as a "not very extravagant hypothesis" alerts us to the possibility that he may in the future expand this hypothesis from a thesis about human psychological reality to something more comprehensive: a thesis about reality as a wider whole.

This is what we find in Chesterton's *Blake*. By the time of writing *Blake* Chesterton's rallying to metaphysical realism was that much more advanced, or at any rate, more articulate. Speaking of mediaeval illuminations, for instance, he writes that "the Christian decorators, being true mystics, were chiefly concerned to maintain the reality of objects."[222]

As we saw in chapter 1 of this study, Chesterton used his Blake book to attack Impressionism, which in a comparison with Gothic

[219]*G. F. Watts*, 53.
[220]Ibid., 54.
[221]Ibid., 61.
[222]*William Blake*, 135.

art he now identifies as scepticism: "It means believing one's immediate impressions at the expense of one's more permanent and positive generalisations."[223]

Here Blake is definitely on the side of the mediaevals: he believed in essential realities, that is, in realities whose ontic outlines were as clear as his own draughtsmanship. Chesterton then surprises us by offering as an example, taken evidently from Blake's "Tyger, tyger, burning bright," the following instance: "an eternal tiger who rages and rejoices for ever in the sight of God."[224] I do not know whether the Oxford Inkling Charles Williams read and was struck by this comment, but his Christian-Platonist fantasy *The Place of the Lion* also posits archetypal realities in the divine creative mind which have their finite counterparts in the creaturely world.[225] Certainly Williams had read a lot of Chesterton, lamenting of him in 1936, "The last of my Lords is dead."[226] Chesterton's Blake and Williams seem as closely associated here as are lions and tigers.

By 1910, when writing *Blake*, Chesterton had himself accepted a form of Christian orthodoxy, and consequently a doctrine of biblical inspiration, which as an Anglo-Catholic theologian of the generation after Chesterton's, Austin Farrer, had argued was in important part a revelation of images.[227] A key image in the last book of the biblical canon, the Johannine Apocalypse, is the Lamb of God, an image of Christ in his divine as well as human reality.

[223] Ibid., 138.

[224] Ibid., 137.

[225] C. Williams, *The Place of the Lion* (London, 1931). Williams was drawing on the later Platonist tradition, subsequently Christianised as a doctrine of the divine Ideas. But then so also was Blake.

[226] Cited in A. S. Dale, *The Outline of Sanity*, 253.

[227] A. Farrer, *The Glass of Vision* (London, 1948).

Chesterton, insisting that Blake's symbols are not allegories, writes that for Blake: "There really is behind the universe an eternal image called the Lamb, of which all living lambs are merely the copies or the approximation."[228] Whereas in Chesterton's discussion of Watts's *Mammon* a naturally occurring reality made manifest in the allegorical painting is symbolised in the paraphernalia and processes of commerce, here a divine reality is manifested in naturally occurring realities, with the connexion between the two disclosed in the biblical symbol.

Commenting on the Johannine notion of the "wrath of the Lamb," Chesterton adds:

> If there is an immortal Lamb, a being whose simplicity and freshness are for ever renewed, then it is truly and really a more creepy idea to horrify that being into hostility than to defy the flaming dragon or challenge darkness or the seas . . .[229]

All of these — dragons, darkness, the seas — are biblical tropes for dangerous cosmic powers that can serve as instruments of divine justice. For Blake, the meekness that is no mere willingness to make oneself a doormat for the feet of others was itself a shadow of the everlasting Lamb.

This brings Chesterton to a marked contrast between Blake and Watts. The atmosphere of Watts's work was, Chesterton tells us, "the belief that abstract verities remained the chief affairs of men when theology left them."[230] In that atmosphere of "sceptical idealism," the use of personal language for divine reality must be

[228]*William Blake*, 141.

[229]Ibid., 142.

[230]*G. F. Watts*, 18.

construed as only figurative. What such language figures is the impersonal, as in the concepts of beauty, truth, goodness. This is far from being the case with Blake or Chesterton himself. Writing in his own name, Chesterton claims that in such language "the impersonal is a clumsy term for something more personal than common personality. God is not a symbol of goodness. Goodness is a symbol of God."[231]

Standing back now from the studies of Watts and Blake, we can seek to square our findings with Chesterton's philosophy of created things by saying that he sought to practice metaphysics through a synthesis of philosophy and mythopoetic thought. It will be a key claim of the closing Christological sections of *The Everlasting Man* that the Incarnation of the Word makes possible precisely such a union of a philosophy and mythopoeisis: a universal philosophy that abstracts from concrete things in the search for general and underlying structures, on the one hand, and on the other, a mythopoetic imagination that discerns divine presence and action as the matrix of the most important concrete things.

Conclusion

For Chesterton, created nature in the cosmos both reveals God and conceals him. God plays a game of hide-and-seek with us in nature, in the world he has made. That is part of the meaning of the elusive, larger-than-life figure of Sunday in *The Man Who Was Thursday*. The key to that novel is that the men who represent cosmic order in society are pursued, harried, by those who suppose them to be really anarchists. In this way, the representatives of order who police the world for its health and safety are able to bear witness that they too have suffered, and this gives them a

[231] *William Blake*, 142.

moral *cachet* in the eyes of all who consider themselves the victims of order. When Syme asks Sunday whether *he* has ever suffered, Sunday's face "grew larger and larger, filling the whole sky, then everything went black." The novel continues: "Only in the blackness before it entirely destroyed his brain he seemed to hear a distant voice saying a commonplace text that he had heard somewhere, 'Can ye drink of the cup that I drink of?' "[232]

---

[232] *The Man Who Was Thursday*, 191. It is only fair to record, against my interpretation, that Chesterton himself, writing a quarter of a century later, described Sunday as "not so much God . . . as Nature as it appears to the pantheist, whose pantheism is struggling out of pessimism" (*Autobiography*, 98). The crux, to my mind, lies in whether one interprets the novel from its prehistory, where its "nightmare" quality ("A Nightmare" was the original subtitle) derives from Chesterton's own struggle out of Slade School madness to incipient faith, or, alternatively, from its time of publication (1908), when Chesterton had made the transition to doctrinal Christianity, as the exactly contemporaneous *Orthodoxy* shows.

Chapter 4

⤳

The Role of Paradox

If in a word-association exercise, someone well versed in English literature were asked to continue a sequence beginning "Chesterton" and "theology," it would be a fair guess that they would offer as answer: "paradox." Chesterton has suffered from this commonplace. The word "paradox" is often taken to mean sheer self-contradiction. More philosophically, it may be taken to be a synonym for "antinomy," meaning: an unavoidable self-contradiction, which is even worse. To say that sheer self-contradiction is intellectually unavoidable is a recipe for philosophical anarchy. The law of non-contradiction is a foundational principle of rational thought. Famously, Hegel queried it, but it needs to be remembered that when Hegel treats of logic he is really dealing with ontology, so in this context what concerns him is clashing tendencies in natural or cultural development. Hegel was not an irrationalist, nor — it should be said without further ado — was Chesterton. Readers of the Father Brown stories may recall that in "The Blue Cross" one of the ways in which Brown is able to unmask the arch-criminal Flambeau, who has disguised himself as a priest, is that Flambeau questions the universality of reason in all possible planetary systems circling the myriads of stars. As Flambeau remarks:

[T]hese modern infidels appeal to their reason, but who can look at those millions of worlds and not feel that there may be wonderful universes above us where reason is utterly unreasonable?[233]

After the capture, Brown explains, "He attacked reason . . . It's bad theology."[234] So Chesterton was certainly not against the use of reason. He only wanted to know *how* reason was being used. As he remarked in his study of the early-nineteenth-century English social critic William Cobbett: "There is nothing very much the matter with the age of reason; except, alas, that it comes before the age of discretion."[235] Hilaire Belloc considered critics had done Chesterton a disservice by naming him a "Master of Paradox," where the word "paradox" is meant to imply a sheer contradiction which baffles reason. Rather, remarked Belloc, at Chesterton's hands paradox was "illumination through an unexpected juxtaposition."[236] That is an important part of the picture, but it is not by any means, as we shall see, all that can be said on this topic.

Paradox is certainly a ubiquitous feature of Chesterton's *oeuvre*. In *Saint Thomas Aquinas*, for instance, Chesterton offers his readers prime examples in succeeding chapters. In chapter I, he tells us, referring to the incarnationalism of both Francis of Assisi and Aquinas, that "these two saints saved us from Spirituality: a dreadful doom."[237] In chapter II, comparing Thomas with his family, who thought his talents would be wasted as a penniless friar, he

---

[233] *The Complete Father Brown Stories*, 28.

[234] Ibid., 32.

[235] *William Cobbett*, 115.

[236] H. Belloc, *On the Place of Gilbert Chesterton in English Letters* (London, 1940), 21.

[237] *Saint Thomas Aquinas*, 21.

affirms the "much more practical pertinacity of the man who is called theoretical."[238] In chapter III, comparing the Aristotle who "took things as he found them" with the Aquinas who "accepted things as God created them," Chesterton infers that Thomas "saved the human element in Christian theology . . . Only, as has already been urged, the human element is also the Christian one."[239] Congruently with this trio of paradoxes he concludes, in chapter IV, which deals with Manicheism, that "the work of heaven alone was material; the making of a material world. The work of hell is entirely spiritual."[240]

A Short History of Attitudes
Toward Chestertonian Paradox

Chesterton was early castigated for over-egging the pudding. One reviewer of *Heretics* remarked:

Paradox ought to be used like onions to season the salad. Mr Chesterton's salad is all onions. Paradox has been defined as "truth standing on her head to attract attention." Mr Chesterton makes truth cut her throat to attract attention.[241]

Probably those critics are correct who suggest that Chesterton learned the habit of paradox from Oscar Wilde, who used it with a like flamboyance. Association with the decadents of *The Yellow Book* — hierophants of a shimmering wit divorced from truth by the simple declaration "art for art's sake" — did nothing to assist

---

[238] Ibid., 48.

[239] Ibid., 66.

[240] Ibid., 85. I owe this chain of references to Y. Denis, G. K.Chesterton: Paradoxe et Catholicisme (Paris, 1978), 17.

[241] Cited in M. Ward, Gilbert Keith Chesterton, 155.

G. K. Chesterton, Theologian

Chesterton's reputation as a serious philosopher, much less as a theologian. That George Bernard Shaw also used the paradox form in the dialogue of his plays may, up to a point, have sweetened that particular pill.

Some help was at hand, however, a decade or so after his death. Chesterton seems always to have been popular in Canada, so perhaps it is not surprising that this aid took the form of the Canadian Hugh Kenner's study, *Paradox in Chesterton*. Published in 1948, Kenner's book argues that for Chesterton paradox is a particularly striking way of bringing home to people the implications of the Thomist doctrine of analogy. According to that doctrine, *likeness with difference* is the all-pervasive feature of relations between creatures as well as between creation (creatures as a whole) and God.

Paradox in Chesterton boasted an introduction by Kenner's fellow-countryman Herbert Marshall McLuhan. McLuhan would become a cult figure of the 1960s, when his maxim, "The medium is the message," more repeated, perhaps, than analysed, was held to sum up the cultural revolution of the period. Oddly, McLuhan's introduction sought to reverse rather than reinforce the message of Kenner's book. While agreeing with Kenner that Chesterton was a major thinker, McLuhan wanted to prize apart the moral metaphysics of Chesterton's doctrine from their literary form, to which paradox is central. For the McLuhan of the 1940s, at any rate, the Chestertonian medium was definitely not the Chestertonian message. McLuhan considered that a deficient, indeed tiresome, literary medium got in the way of a worthwhile moral message in Chesterton's writing.

If McLuhan somewhat shot Kenner in the foot, things looked different thirty years later with the publication in 1978 of a much fuller study in French, *G. K. Chesterton: Paradoxe et Catholicisme*, by Yves Denis. Unlike Kenner's, Denis's book is more theological than philosophical. It locates Chesterton somewhere between the Gospels and such theological giants of *la nouvelle théologie* as the Swiss dogmatician Hans Urs von Balthasar and his French Jesuit mentor Henri de Lubac. As Denis points out, the Jesus of the Gospels himself speaks in paradoxes in key sayings on those who would save their life losing it and those who lose it on his account saving it, on the meek who will possess the earth, on the first being last, or those who want to be greatest of all needing to become the least of all. As to de Lubac, anyone wishing to attempt a reconstruction of his thought would have to take into account two sets of reflections entitled *Paradoxes* and *Nouveaux Paradoxes*.[242] That Balthasar, who regarded de Lubac as his master, had learned from him in this regard becomes apparent when we consider so central a sentence for his theological aesthetics as this one from the opening volume of *The Glory of the Lord*: "All the paradoxes of the being of man and of the world resolve themselves around a centre . . . [which is none other than] the divine obscurity making itself manifest in Jesus Christ."[243] After this demonstration that the paradoxical has its place both in the teaching of the Founder of Christianity and in that of some of the most theologically able among his later-twentieth-century followers, Denis seeks to display the wide ramifications of Chesterton's uses of paradox: pedagogically, doctrinally, mystically, aesthetically. Along with Kenner's, his study remains foundational for later attempts to understand Chesterton's *modus operandi* in this regard.

[242]H. de Lubac, *Paradoxes* (Paris, 1946); idem., *Nouveaux Paradoxes* (Paris, 1955).

[243]H. U. von Balthasar, *La Gloire et la croix. Aspects esthétiques de la Révélation I. Apparition* (Paris, 1965), 409, cited in Y. Denis, *G. K. Chesterton: Paradoxe et Catholicisme*, 19.

G. K. Chesterton, Theologian

The Rhetorical Paradox

What, then, *did* Chesterton intend by multiplying his paradoxes? In part, Chesterton made a selection from a variety of possible rhetorical tools, and among them found paradox especially to his liking. His love of word-play, manifested in enthusiasm for puns and jokes in general, sufficiently explains this. The purpose in his purely rhetorical paradoxes is the maximisation of impact, the securing of effect. As Kenner writes:

> The special rhetorical purpose of Chesterton is to overcome the mental inertia of human beings, which mental inertia is constantly landing them in the strange predicament of both seeing a thing and not seeing it . . . Now a man's acquaintance with truth is likely to be renewed by the violent shock of being told a thundering and obvious lie.[244]

And Kenner cites as an example this passage from Chesterton's *William Blake*:

> Blasphemy is not wild; blasphemy is in its nature prosaic. It consists in regarding in a commonplace manner something which other and happier people regard in a rapturous and imaginative manner.[245]

There is, of course, an obvious sense in which the first proposition in this statement is false: considered as a denial of the divine Goodness, blasphemy *is* wild, wildly off target. But when at any rate *conventional* blasphemy is considered in its contrast to the tropes of Scripture, hymnography, and mystical theology, its imaginative deficiencies, as Chesterton points out, soon become plain.

---

[244]H. Kenner, *Paradox in Chesterton*, 43.
[245]*William Blake*, 178.

Paradox flung out in flat contradiction of the reader may be, as here, a rhetorical device. But it may also be a quite straightforward statement of a contrary case, as Denis explains by reference to Chesterton's study *George Bernard Shaw*.[246] In one sense, declares Chesterton, wherever Shaw counters a commonly received opinion — in Greek, *doxa* — he utters what people insist on calling paradox. To attack head-on an idea in possession which itself appears to be normative, to enjoy the force of intellectual law, may be to *seem* paradoxical. In one of his *Daily News* articles for 1911, Chesterton issued the following advice to any reader in this situation:

> When next you hear some attack called an "idle paradox," ask after the "dox"; ask how long the "dox" has been in the world; how many nations or centuries have believed in the "dox"; how often the "dox" has proved itself right in practice; how often thoughtful men have returned to the "dox" in theory. Pursue the "dox." Persecute the "dox"; in short, ask the "dox" whether it is orthodox.[247]

But secondly, Shaw can also utter judgments whose terms are in collision, and yet any contradiction between them only exists for a superficial mind that contents itself with some current acceptation of terms, ignoring the richness of meaning human language can yield. The role of paradox here is to open thought to a subjacent truth. Chesterton's paradox about blasphemy from his Blake book can illustrate that as well as any Shavian epigram.[248]

[246] Y. Denis, *G. K. Chesterton: Paradoxe et Catholicisme*, 96-98, by way of examination of *George Bernard Shaw*, 76-77.

[247] Cited in M. Ffinch, *G. K. Chesterton*, 87.

[248] Their "talents were strikingly similar but [their] beliefs were so diametrically different": W. B. Furlong, *Shaw and Chesterton. The*

What is distinctive vis-à-vis Shaw in Chesterton's deployment of the rhetorical paradox is twofold. First, it aims at what Platonists term *anamnêsis*, the awakening of unregistered acquaintance, or what Father Brown in "The Three Tools of Death" calls "that strange light of surprise in which we see for the first time things we have known all along."[249] And secondly, such deployment of the rhetorical paradox often serves as, in Denis's term, "a pedagogy for man on his way to the new vision of faith."[250] But while paradox at the hands of Shaw may be comparable to the rhetorical paradox as employed by Chesterton, Shaw does not reach — does not seek to reach — the level of another sort of paradox in Chesterton's writing, a sort with which any consideration of Chesterton as theologian will chiefly be concerned.

What Kenner terms "rhetorical" paradox is what Denis calls "pedagogical" paradox, and these two critics are in agreement that this is the less interesting aspect of the role of paradox in Chesterton's writing, though they also admit it is not always easy to disentangle it from the aspect they rate more highly. This more exalted form of paradox Kenner dubs the "metaphysical" paradox, while Denis gives it the sobriquet the "doctrinal paradox."

Such metaphysical or doctrinal paradoxes are the more important because, at Chesterton's hands, they claim to identify elements in objective reality, rather than constituting simply a choice of stylistic means to bring about a certain effect in reading. These are the paradoxes which in *Orthodoxy* Chesterton terms the primary truths of his theology, what he calls combinations of "two almost insane positions which yet somehow amounted to

Metaphysical Jesters (University Park, Pennsylvania; and London, 1970), 188.

[249] *The Complete Father Brown Stories*, 176.

[250] Y. Denis, *G. K. Chesterton: Paradoxe et Catholicisme*, 155.

sanity."[251] He wants to show how two seemingly incompatible realities, which are supposed to be rebarbative in each other's regard — here opposite poles do not attract but repel — can come together not in some weak compromise but, as he puts it, at the "top of their energy."[252] Judging by the evidence of *Orthodoxy*, what alerted Chesterton to the crucial importance of the metaphysical or doctrinal paradox was his growing realisation that the only humanly fitting way to live in the world is to be at one and the same time passionately optimistic about it (which he interprets to mean passionately loyal) and passionately pessimistic (which he interprets to mean passionately concerned to heal and transform it), and that Christianity alone, by its complex doctrine of creation, fall, and redemption licenses this combination: what he terms "love and wrath both burning."[253]

Such doctrinal paradoxes belong to one or another of two orders. The first such order (and it is the order with which Kenner's book is more concerned) is the order of metaphysical realism. The second relevant order (and here is the focus of Denis's study) is the order of the religious foundation for metaphysical realism. There are, then, two possibilities here. Either doctrinal paradox may concern the world of things and especially of man, as in metaphysical realism, or it may concern God, the realm of the divine, and so the religious foundation for metaphysical realism. Taken broadly, this is, then, a distinction between what would generally be regarded as philosophical and theological subject-matters, but it is relevant to note that a philosophical subject-matter can be approached from either a philosophical or a theological perspective.

[251] *Orthodoxy*, 132.
[252] Ibid., 133.
[253] Ibid.

G. K. Chesterton, Theologian

A foundational doctrinal paradox in the order of metaphysical realism for Chesterton concerns the interrelation of being and nothingness. In his *Saint Francis of Assisi*, Chesterton presents Francis as one who "not only appreciates everything but the nothing of which everything was made."[254] As he writes:

> When we say that a poet praises the whole creation, we commonly mean only that he praises the whole cosmos. But this sort of poet [i.e., a mystical saint like Francis] does really praise creation, in the sense of the act of creation . . . The mystic who passes through the moment when there is nothing but God does in some sense behold the beginningless beginnings in which there was really nothing else.[255]

Somewhat later in the same chapter of that book, denying that Francis was a nature-lover, someone for whom the natural world was a pleasing background environment, Chesterton declares that if Francis's mind had a background, it was, rather, "[t]hat divine darkness out of which the divine love had called up every coloured creature, one by one."[256] The explanation of the philosophical paradox that "everything is made of nothing" is properly theological: plenary divine being has made out of nothing all that is, and only the constant influx of donated being from the giver prevents all things from returning to that nothing from which they were made.

In *Orthodoxy* the foundational ontological paradox is sharpened by the new ontic condition which, alas, is ours, owing to the Fall. In Chesterton's summary, "Whatever I am, I am not myself."[257]

---

[254] *Saint Francis of Assisi*, 87.
[255] Ibid.
[256] Ibid., 98.
[257] *Orthodoxy*, 236.

Created humanity was always suspended between being and nothing, but now, in the post-lapsarian condition, even that genuine being it really receives it holds abnormally. The abnormal is now the norm. Something we have never known in the full sense of that word is not only better than us but is more natural to us than we are to ourselves.[258] And this is why, as he remarks in *Heretics*, if we suppress the supernatural, what we are left with is the counter-natural — an affirmation he will renew in *Orthodoxy*, where it takes the form of saying that only the supernatural can now guard the natural. For *Orthodoxy* this is perhaps the primary paradox offered by the covenant of grace.

> The outer ring of Christianity is a rigid guard of ethical ab-negations and professional priests. But inside that inhuman guard you will find the old human life dancing like children, and drinking wine like men; for Christianity is the only frame for pagan freedom.[259]

The same point was made in poetic form in *The Ballad of the White Horse*, in the song which Alfred sings in the camp of Guthrum, the leader of the pagan Danes:

> *Therefore your end is on you,*
> *Is on you and all your kings,*
> *Not for a fire in Ely Fen,*
> *Not that your Gods are nine or ten,*
> *But because it is only Christian men*
> *Guard even heathen things.*
> *For our God hath blessed creation,*

[258]Ibid.
[259]Ibid., 235.

Calling it good. I know
What spirit with whom you blindly band
Hath blessed destruction with his hand;
Yet by God's death the stars shall stand
And the small apples grow.[260]

Still in the philosophical order of metaphysical realism, another doctrinal paradox highlighted in *Orthodoxy* concerns the
terms on which human nature can flourish. For high-minded paganism in the ancient world, reports Chesterton, that flourishing
was held to consist in some sort of balancing of elements. Here he
appears to have chiefly in mind one interpretation of the Aristotelean doctrine of the virtuous mean. But, Chesterton maintains,
enquiry in depth into the virtues suggests that, to the contrary,
flourishing involves the collision of seemingly opposed passions.
Courage, for instance, one of the four cardinal virtues shared by
antiquity and the Church, consists in a vigorous desire to live taking the form of a disposition to die.[261] Charity, the primary theological virtue, consists of either "pardoning unpardonable acts, or
loving unlovable people."[262]

Once again, the explanation in each case requires us to move
onto the supernatural level: the courage Chesterton has chiefly in
mind is that of the martyrs, who exercise the virtue of courage in
what the mediaeval Scholastics would call an infused form, a form
where the human disposition concerned has already been affected
by grace, while charity, the organising virtue of theological ethics
in Thomism, is, along with faith and hope, an example of an

---

[260]*The Ballad of the White Horse* (London, 1911), 66.

[261]*Orthodoxy*, 134-135.

[262]Ibid., 137.

infused virtue that as such has no "acquired," purely natural, counterpart, in the way that courage does. It is in no way surprising to see Chesterton thinking theologically about the paradoxes presented by forms of human action, anymore than with the paradoxes presented by the interrelation of being and nothingness, since, as Denis rightly sees, the order of metaphysical realism, studied in the first place by philosophy, has for Chesterton its foundation in the realm of the divine, which only theology can study in its own right. Metaphysical realism has a religious foundation.

When we move onto that further order, we find that paradoxes remain pertinent. In classical Christianity, there is a paradoxical interrelation of divine transcendence and divine immanence. Divine transcendence makes possible divine immanence, since it is only inasmuch as God differs from the world that he can be present to it and in it without transgression of the world's inherent character as creation. Transposing that ontological statement into terms of the human knowledge of God, the distance between the divine realm and human understanding which transcendence entails can co-exist, then, with an area of contact between the Creator and created spirit based on the immanence that transcendence makes possible. As Denis puts it, with reference to the book of Deuteronomy: "Like Moses on the threshold of the promised Land the mind glimpses without being able to touch."[263]

By accepting a classical theism for which this is the proper adjudication of the relationship between transcendence and immanence, Chesterton places the chief Christological mysteries — the Incarnation and the Atonement — in a mould of paradox which reflects its character. We can take the Incarnation first. In *The Everlasting Man*, Chesterton takes the midpoint of Christological

[263]Y. Denis, *G. K. Chesterton: Paradoxe et Catholicisme*, 89.

orthodoxy to be the paradoxical combination of the idea of a baby with that of, as he writes, the "unknown strength that sustains the stars."[264] Even in the 1908 *Orthodoxy* Chesterton's Christology, though not so foregrounded, is resolutely Chalcedonian: Jesus Christ is "not a being apart from God and man, like an elf, nor yet a being half human and half not, like a centaur, but both things at once and both things thoroughly, very man and very God."[265]

In *William Blake* he affirmed that in Jesus coincide the "form filling the heavens" and "the appearance of a man."[266]

The paradoxical character of the Incarnation yields further paradoxes in the Atonement. In the temptation scene in the Garden of Olives God tempted God. The cry from the Cross — "Why hast thou forsaken me?" — "confessed that God was forsaken of God."[267] "There is only one religion," remarks Chesterton, "in which God seemed for an instant to be an atheist."[268] Such statements anticipate the most daring theological speculations of Balthasar's theo-dramatic passiology about the self-estrangement of the divine Trinity on the Cross. And the theopaschite formula of the sixth-century Eastern churches seeking to satisfy the element of truth in Monophysitism, "One of the Holy Trinity was crucified for us," receives an even sharper formulation in Chesterton's confession about the death of the Word incarnate in his 1930 independently printed poem "The Grave of Arthur": "Dead is the King who was never born."

And behind these paradoxes of the Incarnation and Atonement lie not only the classical theistic paradoxes of divine transcendence

---

[264] *The Everlasting Man*, 170.

[265] *Orthodoxy*, 133.

[266] *William Blake*, 210.

[267] *Orthodoxy*, 205.

[268] Ibid., 206.

combined with divine immanence, but also the unique paradox at the heart of Nicene orthodoxy which makes possible the dramatic re-expression of inner divine relationships in history: God is a Trinity, or, in Chesterton's words in *Orthodoxy*: "For us Trinitarians (if I may say it with reverence) God Himself is a society."[269]

The Difference Between the
Rhetorical and Metaphysical Paradoxes

The difference between the pedagogical paradoxes and the doctrinal paradoxes is not itself stylistic. As we have seen, Chesterton's aim is sometimes, like Shaw's, simply pedagogical: to jolt minds out of complacency either by briskly denying reigning errors or by conjoining seemingly contradictory terms in order to open thought to a subjacent truth which could be in principle stated in some other way. On other occasions, like those we have just visited, his aim is doctrinal in the strongest sense — namely, to bring people to encounter metaphysical and even more foundationally religious truths in a form which is isomorphic with the realities involved. But in both instances the literary techniques employed are similar: a build-up of argumentation or persuasive discourse is suddenly concentrated in a phrase that shocks. Chesterton introduces what Denis calls "metaphors that initiate," and these set our imagination moving in a certain direction that prepares the reader, subconsciously at any rate, for what is to come: contesting a received opinion and unsettling the reader's mind, often by a humour which arouses tolerance thanks to the pleasurableness of hearing the unaccustomed. But only the crystallisation of the paradox itself, in a sharp formulation of its own, makes the logical impact, bringing together two seemingly contradictory

[269]Ibid., 201.

concepts at the heart of their meaning, thus causing the reader to re-evaluate his or her attitude to truth in some respect as a consequence of a new illumination. Finally, in the characteristic pattern which typifies both pedagogical and doctrinal paradox in Chesterton's prose, imagistic echoes follow, offering some ongoing reminders that return the mind to the focal paradox.

The substance of the distinction between the pedagogical paradox and the doctrinal paradox is not to be found, then, in their literary mechanisms but at another level of analysis.

The Relevance of the "Analogy of Being"

For Hugh Kenner, whose interest lies in Chesterton's use of paradoxes in the order of metaphysical realism, the decisive difference between pedagogical and doctrinal is the tacit presence (or otherwise) of an appeal to the analogy of being, the key doctrine of metaphysical realism in its Thomistic version. For Kenner, this is what enables Chesterton's use of paradox to be not merely rhetorical but fully metaphysical. Kenner states the distinction as follows:

> The object of verbal [i.e., rhetorical] paradox . . . is persuasion, and its principle is the inadequacy of words to thoughts, unless they be very carefully chosen words. But the principle of metaphysical paradox is something inherently intractable in being itself; in the Thing.[270]

And Kenner goes on to say that Chesterton's ultimate object in drawing attention to such metaphysical paradox is eliciting from us "praise, awakened by wonder."[271]

[270]H. Kenner, *Paradox in Chesterton*, 17.
[271]Ibid.

The idea of analogy is that of *likeness at the heart of difference*. This is why analogy thinking is crucial to metaphysics. It is also why it is immediately pertinent to Chesterton's paradoxes in the order of metaphysical realism. In *Heretics* Chesterton invited his readers to realise the "first and simplest of the paradoxes that sit by the springs of truth," namely, to "see that the fact of two things being different implies that they are similar." As he writes:

> The hare and the tortoise may differ in the quality of swiftness, but they must agree in the quality of motion. The swiftest hare cannot be swifter than an isosceles triangle or the idea of pinkness. When we say that the hare moves faster, we say that the tortoise moves. And when we say of a thing that it moves, we say, without need of other words, that there are things that do not move.

And even in the act of saying that things change, we say that there is something unchangeable.[272]

Analogical thinking explains what in the metaphysical order paradox identifies or describes. The common content of analogy and paradox is the intrinsically analogical character of reality: paradox is rooted in being which, by that fact, discloses itself to the metaphysical imagination as wonderful. As Kenner seeks to unfold this point, he writes:

> Everything that is is wrapped in the mystery of its own incommunicable individuality, and hence all things are wonderfully different; but everything that is exercises the act of existence in common with everything else, and in that sense all things are alike. Both the wonder of differentiation and

---

[272]*Heretics*, 46-47.

the wonderful fact of existence are explained and illuminated by the Thomistic ascription of difference to the individual essences of things, in proportion to which they exercise the act of existence. The grass exists grassily, the cloud cloudily; they both are, and they are both different, according to the way in which they are.[273]

That Chesterton understood the main lines of Thomist metaphysics when he wrote his *Saint Thomas Aquinas* is obvious; but Kenner's claim is that years before looking into Thomas, Chesterton's reiterated reports that anything could stimulate him to rapture and elicit the instinct to praise — or example, in one essay, a lamppost[274] — showed that from early manhood on he had always possessed an analogical imagination: that is, an habitually analogical mode of perception. His gratitude was not only that, amid so many potentialities, this particular thing might not have been; it was also that, in its limited being, it participated in the being which has its fount in God.

In the *Autobiography* Chesterton describes his younger self

all groping and groaning and travailing with an inchoate and half-baked philosophy of my own, which was very nearly the reverse of the remark that where there is nothing there is God. The truth presented itself to me, rather, in the form that where there is anything there is God. Neither statement is adequate in philosophy: but I should have been amazed to know how near in some ways was my Anything to the *Ens* of St Thomas Aquinas.[275]

[273] H. Kenner, *Paradox in Chesterton*, 30.
[274] *The Uses of Diversity* (London, 1920), 7.
[275] *Autobiography*, 150.

Chesterton eschewed the language of analogy because, as he explains in *Saint Thomas Aquinas*, he sought to avoid the formal
metaphysical language of the Middle Ages for fear of putting readers off. But he was aware that what made paradox possible was
what allowed the Scholastics to develop their doctrine of analogy:
namely, the non-univocity of key words. Here the Schoolmen
would have singled out most notably the words "one," "good,"
"true," "beautiful," as well as "being" itself. Owing to his decision,
a technical vocabulary was lost to him, but what he added was
humour. The importance of humour in paradox is that it excludes
all explicative commentary that would result in the attenuation of
surprise (and even scandal) in the ontological disclosures that paradox, like analogy, can provide.

For Kenner, Chesterton's Christological incarnationalism capped
or crowned the intuition into the paradoxical character of reality,
a reality whose philosophical explanation he grasped at first tac-
itly and later explicitly as the analogy of being. Any perfection
which man could achieve would be, on the principle of analogy,
infinitely less than God's. Man's littleness, moreover, was intensi-
fied by the Fall, by his sins. Yet on the other hand, man was created
in the divine image, and in the Incarnation God saw fit to assume
that image so as to underline man's greatness, despite the Fall. Par-
adoxically, then, man is both very little and extremely great.[276] In
The Poet and the Lunatics Chesterton ventures the fancy that, as St
Peter was being crucified upside down, he "saw the landscape as it
really is; with the stars like flowers, and the clouds like hills, and
all men hanging on the mercy of God."[277] Certainly this passage

---

[276]H. Kenner, *Paradox in Chesterton*, 93.

[277]*The Poet and the Lunatics: Episodes in the Life of Gabriel Gale* (London, 1929), 27.

supports Kenner's claim, combining a way of looking at the natural cosmos with a view of the existential situation of man in a perspective of sin and grace.

Paradox, Christology, and the Church

Denis's investigation of doctrinal paradox in the wider religious realm which founds the order of metaphysical realism identifies two principal "paradoxes of [Chestertonian] Catholicism." He calls the first "The God-man and the greatness of the little" (a concept that has evident links with Kenner's notion of the Incarnation as the seal of cosmic paradox), and identifies the second as "the Church and the paradoxical universe" (a formulation that has no obvious anticipation in Kenner's study). These two substantive themes will be germane in chapters 7 and 9 respectively, where I deal first with Chesterton's Christology in its own right and finally with Chesterton's account of Catholicism. This latter topic will touch upon the two ways in which, for Denis, Chesterton links paradox with the Catholic style: the "internal balance" and the "festal" character which paradox and Catholicism alike share.

Chapter 5

⤔

The God of Joy

We come now to the quartet of particular theological themes this book will survey: God, man, Christ, and the Church.

A New Argument for the Existence of God?

Chesterton's writings contain what appears to be a novel argument for the existence of God.[278] This argument may be termed the "argument from joy." According to Chesterton, joy as a response to being is the principal signal of transcendence that human experience offers, the most persistent and eloquent of what the sociologist of religion, Peter Berger, has called "rumours of angels."[279]

Joy as Experience

In *The Ballad of the White Horse*, Chesterton suggests that the theme of joy, pervasive in his writings, indicates a kind of aperture in experience: via this aperture we are open to the transcendent

[278]I make use here of some material originally published as Chapter 11 of my book *A Grammar of Consent: The Existence of God in Christian Tradition* (Notre Dame, Indiana, 1991).

[279]P. Berger, *A Rumour of Angels: Modern Society and the Rediscovery of the Supernatural* (London, 1970; Harmondsworth, 1971).

realm that is God. Chesterton speaks of it as a kind of rupture in the chain of cause and effect that governs the finite universe. The passage in question consists of some lines placed in the mouth of the Mother of Jesus and spoken to King Alfred at the darkest point of his struggle with the Danes.

> *I tell you naught for your comfort.*
> *Yea, naught for your desire,*
> *Save that the sky grows darker yet*
> *And the sea rises higher.*
>
> *Night shall be thrice night over you,*
> *And heaven an iron cope.*
> *Do you have joy without a cause,*
> *Yea, faith without a hope.*[280]

The phrase "joy without a cause" is the phrase that I should like to explore further in this chapter.

It may be said at once that by calling joy uncaused, Chesterton did not mean that it was a random or chance occurrence, onto-logically rootless. On the contrary, precisely because, for him, joy is neither empirically bounded nor ethically relevant, its founda-tion must be sought at a deeper level, where the finite opens onto the infinite. Were joy a reaction to empirically specific states or situations, it could be regarded as determined by those states and situations. Were it ethical in content, it could be seen as a reflec-tion of a self-constituted human meaning. But since, as Chester-ton indicates, it is neither of these things, its *raison d'être* must be sought at a point which may be called metaphysical: on the finite-infinite frontier. Joy, he argued, lies deeper than happiness or

---

[280]*The Ballad of the White Horse*, 1.

unhappiness, pleasure or pain. All of these are reactions to particular conditions or events within existence, whereas joy is the reaction to the fact that there should be such a thing as existence at
all. Intimately related to wonder before the fact of being, joy is an
implicit affirmation of the doctrine of creation and hence of the
truth of theism.

Sheer wondering joy before the face of existence is claimed by
Chesterton in the *Autobiography* as a characteristic feature of childhood. The child, he held, sees the world in the light of an eternal
morning that "had a sort of wonder in it as if the world were as new
as myself."[281] Childhood figures prominently in Chesterton's writings for reasons almost directly opposed to those that operate in the
tradition of autobiographical writing at large. Chesterton is virtually uninterested in childhood as the foundational stage of the
individual's psychological development. His study of Stevenson is
an exception to this statement — probably because, on Chesterton's account, Stevenson's experience (toy theatres and all) was so
like his own. Despite sickliness, the grey cityscape of Edinburgh,
and the grim Calvinist or post-Calvinist culture of Scotland, he
could still, at the moment of writing *Treasure Island*, greet existence with at least a "Yo ho ho."[282] For Chesterton childhood is
not significant so much for its contribution to the making of an individual as for its role in disclosing a shared cosmos. In this sense,
he saw it retrospectively as "real life; the real beginnings of what
should have been a more real life; a lost experience in the land of
the living."[283] Far from continuously happy himself as a child, he
maintained that nevertheless, whatever unhappiness and pain

[281] *Autobiography*, 48.

[282] *Robert Louis Stevenson*, 111.

[283] Cited from the Notebooks in M. Ward, *Gilbert Keith Chesterton*, 14.

there might have been were "of a different texture or held on a different tenure."

> What was wonderful about childhood is that anything in it was a wonder. It was not merely a world full of miracles; it was a miraculous world. What gives me this shock is almost anything I recall; not the things I should think most worth recalling.[284]

Yet Chesterton does not regard childhood as a lost fairyland from which adult life is merely an ever-accelerating descent into reality. On the contrary, reality itself in its own utterly non-necessary yet glorious being has the qualities that we normally ascribe to the realm of faëry. For this reason, childhood remains the proper criterion for adult sensibility. The child's response to existence as sheer gift, through wondering joy, is the key to ontology, and, by a supreme irony, far from being a piece of knowledge acquired through the ratiocination of the mature man or woman, it is a gift received with the dawn of consciousness itself. The role of philosophising is to unpack this gift, what elsewhere Chesterton calls this "birthday present" of birth itself,[285] and so to uncover its further implications which lead, in fact, to the postulation of a divine Source for the world. As he wrote in the *Autobiography*, even in a difficult adolescence, "I hung on to the remains of religion by one thread of thanks," being unable to shake off a "sort of mystical minimum of gratitude."[286]

A Philosophy for Joy

Philosophical reflection is also needed to sustain the gift of joy since, as the young Chesterton observed, the experience of living

---

[284] *Autobiography*, 38.

[285] *Orthodoxy*, 73.

[286] *Autobiography*, 94.

in a flawed human environment quickly obscures the sense of joy. Autobiographically, as we noted in chapter 1, Chesterton identified the causes of this abatement of joy as, first, an extreme scepticism, partly brought on by his immersion in the currently fashionable Impressionism, a painterly equivalent (in his view) of epiphenomenalism, and second, a growing sense of the perverse attractiveness of evil, which he associated with his dabblings in spiritualism. He seems to have realised at this juncture that the gift of joy is only of enduring value if, by means of it, the mind can get a sustained hold on the truth of things, *natura rerum*. The rest of his life, in this perspective, is the attempt to work out a philosophy of joy.

Although, at its most conventionally expressed, Chesterton could find this philosophy in the concept of *pulchrum*, the beautiful, a "transcendental" term in Thomism, this was no more than a confirmatory check from the history of Christian philosophy of something that he had been working out more personally in a wide variety of writings. As Marshall McLuhan pointed out, Chesterton did not seek out ideas in the philosophical tradition. Without the apparatus of formal philosophising, he "seems never to have reached any position by dialectic or doctrine, but to have enjoyed a kind of connaturality with every kind of reasonableness."[287] This connatural philosophising, insofar as it touches the subject of joy, can be seen in three of Chesterton's widely separated works.

In his study of Dickens, Chesterton introduces the topic of the gratuitously joy-provoking character of existence by describing Dickens as a man who, if he had learned to whitewash the universe, had done so in a blacking factory.

[287] H. M. McLuhan, "Introduction," in H. Kenner, *Paradox in Chesterton*, xix.

Charles Dickens, who was most miserable at the receptive age when most people are most happy, is afterwards happy when all men weep. Circumstances break men's bones; it has never been shown that they break men's optimism . . . When those who starve or suffer speak for a moment, they do not profess merely an optimism; they are too poor to afford a dear one. They cannot indulge in any detailed or merely logical defence of life; that would be to delay the enjoyment of it. These higher optimists, of whom Dickens was one, do not approve of the universe; they fall in love with it. They embrace life too close to criticise or even to see it. Existence to such men has the wild beauty of a woman, and those love her with most intensity who love her with least cause.[288]

Again, in his masterpiece, *Orthodoxy*, Chesterton speaks of the Christian belief in a God who creates by the communication of his own goodness as the crucial factor in showing the consonance of Christianity with an experientially based ontology:

The mass of men have been forced to be gay about the little things, but sad about the big ones. Nevertheless . . . it is not native to man to be so. Man is more himself, man is more manlike, when joy is the fundamental thing in him and grief the superficial. Melancholy should be an innocent interlude, a tender and fugitive frame of mind; praise should be the permanent pulsion of the soul.[289]

And yet, Chesterton continues:

[288]*Charles Dickens*, 41-42.
[289]*Orthodoxy*, 238.

According to the apparent estate of man, as seen by the pagan or the agnostic, this primary need of human nature can never be fulfilled. Joy ought to be expansive; but for the agnostic it must be concentrated, it must cling to one corner of the world. Grief ought to be a concentration; but for the agnostic its desolation is spread through an unthinkable eternity . . . Christianity satisfies suddenly and perfectly man's ancestral instinct for being the right way up; satisfies it supremely in this: that by its creed joy becomes something gigantic and sadness becomes something special and small.[290]

Finally, in his life of Francis of Assisi, Chesterton refers to joy in the face of existence — ontologically significant joy — as a sign of our relation to the divine creative act. It brings about a kind of contemporaneity with the original creation from nothing.

In a fashion [Francis] endures and answers even the earthquake irony of the Book of Job; in some sense he is there when the foundations of the world are laid, with the morning stars singing together and the sons of God shouting for joy.[291]

Chesterton was well aware that not every reader would be likely immediately to echo this allegedly universal element in the tissue of living. From his earliest writings, Chesterton considered human beings to be in need of a kind of therapy of perception. As he put it in *The Defendant*, "his eyes have changed." P. N. Furbank was right to identify Chesterton's "central belief" in these words:

At the back of our brains . . . there was a forgotten blaze or burst of astonishment at our own existence. The object of

[290] Ibid., 238-239.
[291] *Saint Francis of Assisi* (London, 1923), 87.

the artistic and spiritual life was to dig for this submerged sunrise of wonder.[292]

What Chesterton admires in an artist or writer is, often enough, the ability to cleanse the inner eye from the filming effects of excessive familiarity or of cultural distortion, so that our perceptual limits may approximate more fully to those of integral nature. This is essentially the basis for his veneration of Blake. Admitting that the sentimental classicism of Blake's rival, Thomas Stothard, was sometimes more finely executed in strict painterly terms than Blake's own work, Chesterton adds that this argument reflects "the duel between the artist who wishes only to be an artist and the artist who has the higher and harder ambition to be a man — that is, an archangel."[293] (No doubt Blake's *Songs of Innocence* played a part in confirming Chesterton's view of the significance of joy.[294]) Chesterton belongs to the tradition of philosophy, stretching from Plato to Kierkegaard, which regards rhetoric as a necessary concomitant of argument, precisely because rhetoric can begin to shift certain mental blocks to insight by enlisting the imagination's power to unsettle and reshape consciousness. If all were left to ratiocination alone, such a shift might never occur.

If the poet or artist, sage or saint can elicit this primordial response to being which is joy, then the philosopher can analyse its content. Insofar as Chesterton came in later life to understand and accept Thomism, he seems to have been happy with the Thomist

[292] P. N. Furbank, "Chesterton the Edwardian," in J. Sullivan, ed., *G. K. Chesterton: A Centenary Appraisal* (London, 1974), 21-22, citing from *Autobiography*, 90-91.

[293] *William Blake*, 56.

[294] K. Raine, *William Blake* (London, 1970), 50.

account of beauty as a "transcendental determination of being."[295] Found more systematically in some later Thomists than in Aquinas himself, this concept proposes that a feature of all existent things is their power to arouse our sense of beauty. Finite being in its manifold diversity is, in the words of Yves Denis, "apt for satisfying our entire register for enjoyment."[296] We encounter this deliciousness or radiance in such a variety of beings that the concept that covers it, *pulchrum*, the beautiful, may be termed "transcendental" in the sense of belonging to participation in being at large rather than to a limited set of kinds of being. But because all finite being is received or participated being — because it is not self-explanatory or self-sufficient — the concept of the *pulchrum* becomes one of the ways whereby we may speak of the infinite Source from which the finite realm of being comes forth.[297]

More characteristically Chestertonian, however, is the suggestion that joy may be explained by reference to its correlative concept of gift. The conceptual link is formed by the notion of surprise. Joy is not delight in a settled possession (as in "The Marquis of Lothian enjoys possession of twenty thousand acres"), but delight in what was in itself wholly unexpected — namely, that there should be something at all rather than nothing. It is, therefore, intimately associated with the concept of gift, as a passage in Chesterton's novel *The Poet and the Lunatics* well illustrates.

Man is a creature; all his happiness consists in being a creature; or, as the Great Voice commanded us, in being a child. All his fun is in having a gift or present; which the child,

[295] *Saint Thomas Aquinas*, 175-195.

[296] Y. Denis, G. K. *Chesterton: Paradoxe et Catholicisme*, 37.

[297] Compare J. Maritain, *Creative Intuition in Art and Poetry* (New York, 1954), 160-167.

with profound understanding, values because it is a "surprise." But surprise implies that a thing comes from outside of ourselves; and gratitude that it comes from someone other than ourselves. It is thrust through the letter-box; it is thrown in at the window; it is thrown over the wall. Those limits are the lines of the very plan of human pleasure.[298]

It is in this way that Chesterton's *argumentum e gaudio* proceeds from a certain recurrent feature of human experience, rendered intelligible by reflection about the existence of God. God is the true but hidden centre to which Chesterton alluded when he sought to explain Dickens's "incomparable hunger and pleasure for the vitality and the variety, for the infinite eccentricity of existence."[299] He continues: "We feel that all there is is eccentric, though we do not know what is the centre."[300] The divine centre is off-side. Yet for all that, it makes its presence felt.

No doubt such an argument needs conceptualisation in a setting where other types of theistically suggestive experience are also included and appraised.[301] Nevertheless, it seems as worthy of attention by philosophers as, for instance, the argument from desire found in Gregory of Nyssa, or the argument from hope in Gabriel Marcel, or even the argument *e contingentia mundi* in Aquinas to which, indeed, it might usefully be related.

If an argument for God's existence can be based on the phenomenon of joy, then we are in the presence of one of Chesterton's celebrated paradoxes. It would certainly be paradoxical if a problem

[298] *The Poet and the Lunatics*, 129.

[299] *Charles Dickens*, 286.

[300] Ibid.

[301] I attempted this in the original setting of this chapter: A *Grammar of Assent*.

that has aroused the conceptual and argumentative intricacies of, say, the argument from a First Mover, or the argument from design, were in some sense soluble by reference to what is, on Chesterton's own showing, essentially an infantile emotion. Tiresome as Chesterton's exploitation of paradox may sometimes be, it is justified for him, as our explorations in the last chapter indicated, by considerations based on ontology rather than style. In *Orthodoxy* Chesterton declares a hatred for pure paradox and a love for truth which has, he argues, an objectively extravagant aspect.[302] As Denis writes, "for him paradox is not a mask; it is a disclosure."[303] That the point of insertion of God into the human continuum should be something as simple as joy is a serious suggestion, though made in a playful way. Here as elsewhere, Chesterton's imagination is formidably intellectual. The paradox is not a game; rather, the sense of play is a pleasure arising simultaneously with the paradox from the perceived truth: "The humour is inseparable from the argument. It is . . . the 'bloom' on dialectic itself."[304]

In this connection it is worth returning by way of conclusion to Peter Berger's *A Rumour of Angels*, an essay that Chesterton would undoubtedly have found highly sympathetic. Berger points out that "ludic," playful, elements can be found in virtually every sector of human culture, to such a degree that, so it may be argued, culture as such is impossible without play. Here reference is made to the Dutch historian Jan Huizinga's *Homo Ludens* where these ludic elements can be connected to the theme of joy.[305] Berger writes:

---

[302] *Orthodoxy*, 4-5.

[303] Y. Denis, G. K. *Chesterton: Paradoxe et Catholicisme*, 17.

[304] C. S. Lewis, *Surprised by Joy* (London, 1935, 1939), 143.

[305] J. Huizinga, *Homo Ludens: A Study of the Play Element in Culture* (Boston, 1955).

> Joy is play's intention. When this intention is actually real-
> ised, in joyful play, the time structure of the playful universe
> takes on a very specific quality — namely, it becomes eter-
> nity . . . Even as one remains conscious of the poignant real-
> ity of that other "serious" time in which one is moving
> towards death, one apprehends joy as being, in some barely
> conceivable way, a joy forever.[306]

And from an astonishing concentration of the insights of Chesterton's writings, Berger infers that it is the human being's ludic constitution that enables us to regain and realise the deathless joy of
our childhood. Thus play becomes the anthropological key to joy,
and joy the anthropological key to truth. Can one echo the words
of Denis and agree that Chesterton has found "the gateway to the
land of marvels"?[307]

---

[306] P. Berger, A Rumour of Angels, 76-77.
[307] Y. Denis, G. K. Chesterton: Paradoxe et Catholicisme, 38.

Chapter 6

⌒

Man in the Image of God

The theme of man in the image of God is likely to crop up almost anywhere in Chesterton's writing, sometimes in unlikely places. But that is not really surprising. Chesterton was a wonderfully generous-spirited human being who was worried, with reason, about the present and future condition of his fellowmen; he also accepted the truth of Christianity. The doctrine of the imagehood of God in man is the foundational doctrine of Christian anthropology, and therefore the most important element in Christian truth to have to hand if what is needed is a re-orientation in the sense of the *humanum*: what it is to be human at all, what are the conditions of flourishing of the human, and what is the expected destiny of the human.

Starting from Dickens

Chesterton's most systematic statement of his anthropology is surely the account to be found in the first half of *The Everlasting Man*. I begin, nevertheless, with a statement not from that theological masterwork of his maturity but from his early study of Charles Dickens. I do so partly because it serves to link the last of our fundamental topics — paradox — to this key topic among particular

119

doctrines — namely, theological anthropology. Chesterton has been dealing with the complaint that, in his handling of his characters, and general attitude to the human race, Dickens was, as some critic or another had opined, a "vulgar optimist." Chesterton accords this accusation a measure of truth. As he writes:

> Let us admit that Dickens' mind was far too much filled with pictures of satisfaction and cosiness and repose. Let us admit that he thought principally of the pleasures of the oppressed classes; let us admit that it hardly cost him any artistic pang to make out human beings as much happier than they are.[308]

A curious fact remains. Dickens succeeded in eliminating some of the social wrongs he detested: he brought about some of the reforms in English social institutions that he wanted to see. The explanation, continues Chesterton, is that, like "every real and desirable thing," Dickensian social reform entails a "mystical contradiction."[309] Explaining what particular paradox he has in mind, Chesterton draws near to the doctrine of man as the image of God.

Chesterton's argument runs as follows:

> If we are to save the oppressed, we must have two apparently antagonistic emotions in us at the same time. We must think the oppressed man intensely miserable, and at the same time intensively attractive and important. We must insist with violence upon his degradation; we must insist with the same violence upon his dignity. For if we relax by one inch the one assertion, men will say he does not need saving. And if

---

[308] *Charles Dickens* (London, 1907, fifth edition), 268.
[309] Ibid., 269.

we relax by one inch the other assertion, men will say he is not worth saving. The optimists will say that reform is needless. The pessimists will say that reform is hopeless. We must apply both simultaneously to the same oppressed man; we must say that he is a worm and a god; and must thus lay ourselves open to the accusation (or the compliment) of transcendentalism.[310]

Only if man has been clothed at his creation with divine dignity is it safe to affirm the deplorable condition, physical, moral, and in every other way, sometimes in extreme forms, that can be his on earth. We could not bear to face the facts about human depravity in their stark grimness if human dignity were essentially an earthly dignity, that is, a property of the human animal as such. As Chesterton puts it: "If [human dignity] is a heavenly dignity we can admit the earthly degradation with all the candour of Zola,"[311] a reference to the ultra-realist novelist of French industrial society who sought to shock the bourgeoisie by his tell-all descriptions of the physical and moral squalor of the proletariat, allied in his writing with a deterministic biology of the human taken from his reading of Darwin.

Clearly, it is not simply a question of an inhibition about naming human depravity. It is also a question of the well-foundedness or otherwise of the hope of getting people to cooperate in doing something about it. Chesterton does not name the doctrine of the divine imagehood of man in so many words, but that is what he evidently has in mind when he calls this need to identify the conditions of reform the "strongest argument for the religious conception of

[310]Ibid., 270.
[311]Ibid.

life."³¹² Every man is the bearer of the royal image; he or she is stamped with the seal of the divine King. Human rights, which are the explication, the unfolding, of that intrinsic human dignity, are not so much natural rights as they are supernatural rights — as Chesterton *does* state in so many words, appealing to Thomas Jefferson for confirmation, in *What I Saw in America*.³¹³

The American Example

In the context of our present theme, that book, which dates from the year of his conversion to Catholicism, 1922, deserves some mention. In his retrospect on his tour of the United States, which had occupied the early months of 1921, he declared roundly, "There is no basis for democracy except in a dogma about the divine origin of man."³¹⁴ Chesterton was correct in observing that the growth of such scientific — or perhaps pseudo-scientific — disciplines as craniology, which sought to correlate intelligence with the structure of the skull and both with racial inheritance, had added to the problems of Abolitionists in the ante-bellum epoch in America. He believed that not only would Abolitionism have had the utmost difficulty in establishing itself without the Civil War, itself fought for other reasons, but that, had slavery continued until the end of the century — into the era of what he termed "evolutionary imperialism" — the anthropological basis for its legal removal would no longer have been available. It was against the trend of the nineteenth century that Lincoln reiterated the principal Jeffersonian tenets stated in the founding documents of the American Republic, "We hold these truths to be self-evident; that all

---

³¹²*Charles Dickens*, 270.
³¹³*What I Saw in America*, 153.
³¹⁴Ibid., 305.

men are created equal, that they are endowed by their Creator, etc." Lincoln did so, as Chesterton puts it:

to a generation that was more and more disposed to say something like this: "We hold these truths to be probable enough for pragmatists; that all things looking like men were evolved somehow, being endowed by heredity and environment with no equal rights, but very unequal wrongs," and so on.[315]

Chesterton expresses his doubts as to whether such a creed could ever "have overthrown a slave state."[316]

But what about the creed of Catholic Christianity? Could it do any better? Chesterton does not propose to argue that Christian orthodoxy renders inevitable political democracy and the recognition of universal human rights. A regime issuing from evangelical and Catholic inspiration is, he agrees, "not . . . necessarily at any moment more democratic" than some other. The important point lies elsewhere and consists in the fact that "its indestructible minimum of democracy really is indestructible."[317] And, he goes on:

[B]y the nature of things that mystical democracy was destined to survive, when every other sort of democracy was free to destroy itself. And whenever democracy destroying

---

[315]Ibid., 301-302.

[316]Ibid., 300. "The view that . . . rights are the universal property of men as such was virtually unknown in classical antiquity. Frequently when it is presented even now, there is little comprehension of the *philosophical* difficulties it entails. It is in many respects an ethical survival whose first espousal depended on a now-abandoned theological belief that man was formed in the image of God": thus J. M. Rist, *Human Value: A Study in Ancient Philosophical Ethics* (Leiden, 1982), 1.

[317]*What I Saw in America*, 303.

itself is suddenly moved to save itself, it always grasps at rag or tag of that old tradition that alone is sure of itself.[318]

For Chesterton, Enlightenment humanism is really dependent on a perception deriving ultimately from the biblical account of the creation of the universal proto-parents in the divine image.

Chesterton's conviction that acceptance of a divinely originated dignity for each member of the human species is not only a religious but a moral necessity was from the beginning on a collision course with later-nineteenth-century biological materialism. "Thinking people," he briskly declares in "The Evolution of Slaves," an essay in the collection *Fancies Versus Fads*, know that "the constant flux of adaptation" posited by evolutionary anthropology does not exist.

> So far from saying that the evolution of man has not finished, they will point out that (as far as we know) it has not begun. In all the five thousand years of recorded history, and in all the prehistoric indications before it, there is not a shadow or suspicion of movement or change in the human biological type.[319]

Chesterton's suspicion is that the claim that evolution is ongoing for the human phylum is only too convenient for ideological interventionists who wish to aim the path of the human species in a given direction, of which he offers various examples, the most anodyne of which is vegetarianism. "Having risen from a monkey who eats nuts to a man who eats mutton, [man] may rise yet higher by eating nuts again."[320] The denial that man is properly thought of

---

[318]*What I Saw in America*, 303.

[319]*Fancies Versus Fads* (London, 1923), 183.

[320]Ibid.

as a higher animal will be the true starting point of *The Everlasting Man*, to which I now turn.

The Genesis of The Everlasting Man

Chesterton's *Everlasting Man* was written as a response to *An Outline of History*, a one-man history of the world by his old sparring partner H. G. Wells. What endeared the Wells of Edward VII's reign in Chesterton's eyes was Wells's willingness to admit his mistakes, philosophical and otherwise. This trait survived into the reign of George V. The First World War derailed the juggernaut of Wellsian progress and punctured the confidence Wells had fluctuatingly shown in the inevitably ameliorative effects of science. Chesterton would not live long enough to witness the sorry spectacle of the Wells of the years immediately following the Second World War, the War of Holocaust and Hiroshima, and so missed the despairing reaction of Wells's study *Mind at the End of Its Tether*.

What Chesterton noted about *An Outline of History* were two things. First, Wells took it for granted that the human being was simply the product of mammalian development along a particular evolutionary track. Secondly, Wells gave minimal space to Christ and the Gospel: his section on Jesus of Nazareth occupied only a quarter the length of his account of the struggles of the ancient Greeks with the Persian empire, and, like Christianity itself, Christ became invisible in Wells's scenario as soon as Wells left the mediaeval period behind, something he did very expeditiously.[321]

The central thesis of *The Everlasting Man* is that the two chief axes of history are missing in Wells's account. What one ought to note about human history is, in the first place, the rupture in the

---

[321] I follow here the account of the book's origins in S. L. Jaki, *Chesterton, A Seer of Science*, 61.

natural continuum produced by the emergence of *homo sapiens*, and, in the second place, the unique transformation of human possibilities that was displayed by the Incarnation. When cut along its most significant internal boundary-lines, history breaks down, accordingly, into two phases. It is anthropophany, followed by Christophany. What an outline of history should offer above all is, first, an account of the creative explosion with which man arrives on the animal scene, followed by, secondly, an account of the figure who represents a unique qualitative leap in human experience. Neither of these manifestations can be explained naturalistically; both of them submit only to theological explication.

The Divine Origin of Man

When we consider the reality of man in the image of God, we are concerned with the first of these two claims. Chesterton addresses this claim in his essay "The Secret Society of Mankind" (also included in *Fancies Versus Fads*):

> The truth involved here has had many names; that man is the image of God; that he is the microcosm; that he is the measure of all things. He is the microcosm in the sense that he is the mirror, the only crystal we know in which the fantasy and fear in things are, in the double and real sense, things of reflection.[322]

Incidentally, Chesterton reiterates the democratic implications of that statement when he rounds it off by remarking:

> In the presence of this mysterious monopoly the differences of men are like dust. That is what the equality of men means

---

[322] *Fancies Versus Fads*, 122-123.

to me, and that is the only intelligible thing it ever meant to anybody.[323]

The Everlasting Man, then, in its two diptychs, anthropological and Christological, opens by explaining the method Chesterton will follow. That method is to look at his two subject-matters, the human and the Christian, by the strongest imaginative effort that can be made to see both *as if from the outside*. So far as the human being goes, it is, specifically, by seeing man as a strange animal that we shall realise "how strange an animal he is."[324] It is, in Chesterton's words, "exactly when we do regard man as an animal that we know he is not an animal."[325] Compared with animal nature, so Chesterton hopes to show, "man has distanced everything else with a distance like that of the astronomical spaces and a speed like that of the still thunderbolt of the light."[326] Chesterton had no objection to the theory of evolution insofar as it postulated the gradual character of the formation of non-human species by natural selection. Yet he was keenly aware of the problem created for Darwinism by the surprising paucity of the transitional forms that the theory seemed to require, and thus treated it as an hypothesis. Questions of the length of evolutionary time he dismissed as "a merely relative question of the same story being spun out or rattled rapidly through, as can be done with any story at a cinema by turning a handle."[327] Nor did he object to the application of Darwinian concepts to the development of the human

[323] Ibid., 123.
[324] *The Everlasting Man*, 16.
[325] Ibid., 17.
[326] Ibid., 19.
[327] Ibid., 26.

body. His chief objection was to the notion that Darwinism could explain the human soul — the distinctively human configuration of consciousness and activity. The distance between man and the other animals is simply too great for this to be plausible.

A subsidiary but still important ancillary objection is to the notion that the prehistory of human evolution has any predictive power for the future of mankind. Were we to take one statement from *The Descent of Man* which encapsulated what Chesterton disliked about evolutionary biology, it would be when Darwin writes by way of conclusion:

> Man may be excused at feeling some pride at having risen, though not through his own exertions, to the very summit of the organic scale; and the fact of his having thus risen, instead of having been aboriginally placed there, may give him hope for a still higher destiny in the distant future.[328]

The denial of aboriginal placement; the flagging up of the possibility of an evolutionist eschatology: these are the errors, and they are no bagatelle because they concern, literally, the *alpha* and the *omega* of the human creature: its first beginning and its last end.

Man Is a Revolution

As Chesterton notes, these fundamental issues of human origin will not be decided aright unless we bring to the fore the fact that "man is not merely an evolution but rather a revolution."[329] For Chesterton, the first telltale sign of this revolution is that man is an animal who paints. Hence the beginning of his account

[328]C. Darwin, *The Descent of Man* (London, 1882, second edition), 619.

[329]*The Everlasting Man*, 26.

in a cave, that is, one of the caves in southwestern France and northern Spain in which the best preserved Palaeolithic artworks can be viewed (by select professionals, at any rate) owing to the fragility of the micro-climates that sustain the pigmentation. The Altamira caves were opened up in 1878, those of Font de Gaume, which confirmed the authenticity of the Altamira paintings, in 1903, and in 1940, four years after Chesterton's death, the best-known of all, the caves of Lascaux, in the Dordogne. One curiosity of Chesterton's 1925 account is that he waxes lyrical on the circumstance of the discovery of cave-art by "a priest and a boy." This description does not tally with either Altamira or Font de Gaume; but of the first four people to enter the caves of Lascaux, so Stanley Jaki reports, two were boys and one was a priest.[330] Make of that what one will, what seems clear is that for later-twentieth-century students of Palaeolithic art, its emergence remains, as in Chesterton's account, explosively sudden: one enquiry into the origins of art from the 1980s is entitled *The Creative Explosion*.[331]

Chesterton imagines a visit to inspect this artwork by "one of the professors who simplified the relation of men and beasts to a mere evolutionary variation."[332] The professor:

had dug very deep and found the place where a man had drawn the picture of a reindeer. But he would dig a good deal deeper before he found a place where a reindeer had drawn a picture of a man.

[330]S. L. Jaki, *Chesterton, A Seer of Science*, note 23, 142.

[331]J. E. Pfeiffer, *The Creative Explosition: An Inquiry into the Origins of Art and Religion* (New York, 1982).

[332]*The Everlasting Man*, 32.

Chesterton calls this a "tremendous truth." The professor might

> descend to depths unthinkable, he might . . . see in those
> cold chasms or colossal terraces of stone, traced in the faint
> hieroglyphic of the fossil, the ruins of lost dynasties of bio-
> logical life . . . He would find the trail of monsters blindly
> developing in directions outside all our common imagery of
> fish and bird; groping and grasping and touching life with
> every extravagant elongation of horn and tongue and ten-
> tacle; growing a forest of fantastic caricatures of the claw
> and the fin and the finger. But nowhere would he find one
> finger that had traced one significant line upon the sand;
> nowhere one claw that had even begun to scratch the faint
> suggestion of a form.[333]

Defining art as "the notion of reproducing things in shadow or representative shape," Chesterton asks us to note that the evidence carries no hint of a development of artistic skills from the rudimentary in animals to the more evolved in ourselves.

> Monkeys did not begin pictures and men finish them.
> Pithecanthropus did not draw a reindeer badly and Homo
> sapiens draw it well. The higher animals did not draw better
> and better portraits; the dog did not paint better in his best
> period than in his early bad period as a jackal; the wild
> horse was not an Impressionist and the race horse a Post-
> Impressionist.[334]

If man was "an ordinary product of biological growth," then he was not like any other.

---

[333]*The Everlasting Man*, 33.
[334]Ibid., 34-35.

Indeed, remarks Chesterton, he "seems rather more supernatural as a natural product than as a supernatural one."[335] The right conclusion to be drawn is that:

> somehow or other a new thing had appeared in the cavernous night of nature, a mind that is like a mirror. It is like a mirror because it is truly a thing of reflection. It is like a mirror because in it alone all the other shapes can be seen like shining shadows in a vision. Above all, it is a mirror because it is the only thing of its kind. Other things may resemble it or resemble each other in various ways; other things may excel it or excel each other in various ways; just as in the furniture of a room a table may be round like a mirror or a cupboard larger than a mirror. But the mirror is the only thing that can contain them all. Man is the microcosm; man is the measure of all things; man is the image of God.[336]

If we look at man in the company of the animals, we have to say he is a "very strange being," almost a "stranger on the earth."[337] He wraps himself in "artificial bandages called clothes"; he props himself on "artificial crutches called furniture." He hides his own organs of generation "as in the presence of some higher possibility which creates the mystery of shame." And alone among the animals, he is "shaken with the beautiful madness called laughter."[338]

That was a point Chesterton had already made in criticism of the Irish agnostic man of letters George Moore. Moore had proposed that comedy and tragedy, the inherent possibilities of

[335] Ibid., 35.
[336] Ibid.
[337] *The Everlasting Man*, 36.
[338] Ibid.

humour as well as the ever-present shadow of mortality, belong equally with all that lives: in Moore's words, "whether it be leviathan or butterfly, oak or violet, worm or eagle." Chesterton drew to his attention what he called the "prodigious fact" that man is the only creature that actually laughs, besides which, he remarked, "the fact that men laugh in different degrees, and at different things, shrivels not merely into insignificance but into invisibility.[339] In his essay on Moore, "The Secret Society of Mankind," Chesterton writes:

> It is true that I have often felt the physical universe as something like a firework display: the most practical of all practical jokes. But if the cosmos is meant for a joke, men seem to be the only cosmic conspirators who have been let into the joke.[340]

Citing Moore's own catalogue of creatures:

> We may come upon him in some quiet dell rolling about in uproarious mirth at the sight of a violet. But we shall not find the violet in a state of uproarious mirth at Mr Moore. He may laugh at the worm; but the worm will not turn and laugh at him. For that comfort he must come to his fellow sinners . . .

In *The Everlasting Man*, Chesterton does not include among the differentia of the human our consciousness of mortality, but this played its part in the controversy with Moore, which concerned not only the uniqueness of man in nature but also the spiritual equality, despite other inequalities, of the members of the

[339]*Fancies Versus Fads*, 122.
[340]Ibid.

human species: what Chesterton calls the "solidarity and sameness of mankind."[341] Whereas all living things die, only man knows that he will. Asks Chesterton:

> Can Mr Moore draw forth leviathan with a hook, and extract his hopes and fears about the heavenly harpooner? Can he worm its philosophy out of a worm, or get the caterpillar to talk about the faint possibility of a butterfly? The caterpillar on the leaf may repeat to Blake his mother's grief; but it does not repeat to anybody its own grief about its own mother.[342]

And he goes on:

> We do not know what a whale thinks of death; still less of what the other whales think of his being killed and eaten. He may be a pessimistic whale, and be perpetually wishing that this too, too solid blubber would melt, thaw and resolve itself into a dew. He may be a fanatical whale, and feel frantically certain of passing instantly into a polar paradise of whales, ruled by the sacred whale who swallowed Jonah. But we can elicit no sign or gesture from him suggestive of such reflections; and the working common sense of the thing is that no creatures outside man seem to have any sense of death at all.[343]

Only a human death can be a tragedy, from which flow "all the forms and tests" whereby we further characterise it as murder or execution, martyrdom or suicide: all these depend "on an echo or

[341] Ibid., 121.
[342] Ibid., 120.
[343] *Fancies Versus Fads*, 121.

vibration, not only in the soul of man, but in all the souls of all men,"[344] precisely because all know the shadow of death falls on them.

Biological Archaeology or Meta-history?

For Chesterton there may be a "broken trail of stones and bones faintly suggesting the development of the human body," but there is "nothing even faintly suggesting such a development of the human mind."[345] As he writes: "Something happened; and it has all the appearance of a transaction outside time. It has therefore nothing to do with history in the ordinary sense."[346] The original human ensoulment is a meta-historical event which renders human history possible: taking the word "history" to stand for both the sequence of events in the human past and the study of those events by historians. The historian must take something like it for granted; he cannot investigate it, any more than can the biologist.

The Fall and Original Sin

Chesterton took the same view of Original Sin, when welcoming Aldous Huxley's departure from the view of such late Victorian and Edwardian rationalists as his father, Thomas Huxley, that acceptance of the doctrine of Original Sin was an unnecessarily cramping limitation to one's estimate of the human species. Unfortunately, for Chesterton, the younger Huxley then rather spoiled things by adding that "the scientific view of man necessitates a sort of original sin, if it be only the residuum of his animal

---

[344] *Fancies Versus Fads*, 121.
[345] Ibid., 38.
[346] Ibid.

ancestry."[347] "Sin, whatever else it is," declared Chesterton in his essay "On Original Sin," reprinted in the collection *Come to Think of It*, "is not merely the dregs of a bestial existence." Rather, it is "something more subtle and spiritual." Indeed, it is "in some way connected with the very supremacy of the human spirit." As he wrote:

> It is not merely a matter of letting the ape and tiger die, for apes are not Pharisees, nor are tigers prigs. The elephant does not turn up his long nose at everything with any superior intention, and the totally unjust charge of hypocrisy might well be resented by any really sensitive and thin-skinned crocodile. The giraffe might be called a highbrow, but he is not really supercilious about the powers of Uplift.[348]

And he complained that, in the moralising literature of bestiaries and fables:

> Man has scattered his own vices as well as virtues very arbitrarily among the animals, and there may be no more reason to accuse the peacock of pride than to accuse the pelican of charity. The worst things in man are only possible to man.[349]

He insists:

> That poison is his own recipe; it is not merely decaying animal matter. That poison is most poisonous where there are fine scientific intellects or artistic imaginations to mix it. It is just as likely to be at its best — that is, at its worst — at the end of a civilization as at the beginning. Of this sort are

[347] Cited in "On Original Sin," in *Come to Think of It*, 156.
[348] Ibid.
[349] Ibid.

all the hideous corruptions of culture; the pride, the perversions, the intellectual cruelties, the horrors of emotional exhaustion. You cannot explain that monstrous fruit by saying that our ancestors were arboreal; save, indeed, as an allegory of the [Genesis] Tree of Knowledge.[350]

So he concludes:

The poison . . . is as old as any memory of man. Wherefore, we have to posit of it that it also was of the human source and fountainhead, that it was in the beginning, or, as the old theology affirms, original.[351]

Actually, both Chesterton's discovery of metaphysical realism and his distinctive argument for the existence of God predisposed him to an acceptance of the dogma of the Fall. As Adam Schwartz explains, Chesterton's conviction that the grateful acceptance of the gift of existence in joyful humility is what leads to happiness received confirmation in "the Christian dogma that it was precisely proud ingratitude and the arrogant ambition of creatures to be like God that precipitated the human race's aboriginal calamity."[352] We shall not perhaps expect so genial a man as Chesterton to write compendiously about vices, but neither shall we be surprised that for him "the true vanity of vanities" is the sin of pride. Pride's subtlety is such that "[a]ll other sins attack men when they are weak and weary; but this attacks when men are happy and valuable and nearer to all the values."[353] Just like Adam, in fact.

---

[350]Cited in "On Original Sin," in *Come to Think of It*, 157.

[351]Ibid.

[352]A. Schwartz, *The Third Spring*, 66.

[353]*The Apostle and the Wild Ducks, and Other Essays*, D. Collins, ed., 13.

At the same time, that doctrine also liberates humankind by its implicit claim that there is nothing fixed about endemic moral defect. To Chesterton's mind, rejection of the dogma of Original Sin entails acceptance of the "persistently flawed state of human nature as normative." That road leads to despair (compare Wells). But if man has fallen from a higher dignity, he may be restored thereto by cooperating with God's grace.[354]

The Defence of Free Will

According to Chesterton, we are free to mix the poisons our spiritual ancestry makes available to us in the way we like, just as we are also free to abstain. He was hardly likely to fall into a theological necessitarianism about personal sin, when he had fought so long and valiantly against philosophical, biological, and psycho-analytic necessitarianisms of various kinds. In an essay "On Psycho-analysis" he absolved the dramatists and poets of the Greco-Roman civilization of any such error.

> Insofar as old tragedy was a struggle between Fate and Free Will, it represented the defeat of Free Will and not the denial of Free Will. The struggle of man against the gods might be a hopeless struggle, but it was a struggle. It is the whole point of modern Determinism that there can be no struggle at all.[355]

Chesterton's blazing affirmations of freedom made him impatient with legal reformers who sought to replace retributory rationales for judicial punishment by alternatives which justified imprisonment, for instance, in terms of protecting society. While it is true

---

[354] A. Schwartz, *The Third Spring*, 67.
[355] *Come to Think of It*, 55.

that we are not infallible when we think we are punishing criminals, it is also true that we are not infallible when we think we are protecting society. When the "Potteries" novelist Arnold Bennett lent his weight to the view that crime is the result of conditioning, so only the rationale of social protection will serve, Chesterton responded vigorously in his ironically entitled essay, "The Mercy of Mr Arnold Bennett."

> Mr. Bennett's solution is not the more merciful, but the less merciful of the two. To say that we may punish people, but not blame them, is to say that we have a right to be cruel to them, but not a right to be kind to them. For after all, blame is itself a compliment. It is a compliment because it is an appeal; and an appeal to a man as a creative artist making his soul . . . [W]hen we call a man a coward, we are in so doing asking him how he can be a coward when he could be a hero. When we rebuke a man for being a sinner, we imply that he has the powers of a saint.[356]

Punishing someone for the protection of society, thought Chesterton, "involves no regard for him at all." Especially, it involves no "limit of proportion" in punishment.

> There are some limits to what ordinary men are likely to say that an ordinary man deserves. But there are no limits to what the danger of the community may be supposed to demand.[357]

The State trials of the Soviet Union would shortly confirm the pertinence of Chesterton's comment. Bennett's intervention was an

[356] *Fancies Versus Fads*, 88, 89.
[357] Ibid., 89.

example of what Chesterton called elsewhere the way in which "the progressive, generation after generation, does elaborately tie himself up in new knots": above all with respect to his picture of man.[358]

In "The Revolt of the Spoilt Child," Chesterton took issue with the newly fashionable philosophy of education and counselling which had as its aim "drawing out the true personality of the child, or allowing a human being to find his real self."[359] The only meaning that can be assigned to "finding one's true self," thought Chesterton, is a matter of mystical theology, and concerns divine purpose in creating. Otherwise, "it is so unmeaning that it cannot be called mystery but only mystification."

> Humanly considered, a human personality is only the thing that does in fact emerge out of a combination of the forces inside the child and the forces outside . . . Anybody might amuse himself by trying to subtract the experiences and find the self; anybody who wanted to waste his time.[360]

In the "case of the finest and most distinguished personalities," Chesterton noted, it would be hard to "disentangle them from the trials they have suffered, as well as from the truths they have found."[361] Chesterton continues:

> God alone knows what the child is really like, or is meant to be really like. All we can do is to fill [the child] with those truths which we believe to be equally true whatever he is like.[362]

[358]"The Revolt of the Spoilt Child," in *Fancies Versus Fads*, 138.
[359]Ibid., 139.
[360]*Fancies Versus Fads*, 139, 140.
[361]Ibid.
[362]Ibid., 140.

So, we must "believe in a religion or philosophy firmly enough to take the responsibility of acting on it."[363]

We have already looked at Chesterton's philosophy. In the next chapter we must consider his Christologically defined religion.

---

[363]*Fancies Versus Fads*, 141.

Chapter 7

Chesterton's Christology

For Chesterton, "the double nature of Christ" is "the essential paradox of the Incarnation."[364] Those words from *Christendom in Dublin* show us how strongly Chalcedonian Chesterton's Christology is. Perhaps an even better term than "Chalcedonian" would be "Leonine," for Chesterton's mature theology of the Incarnation is extraordinarily Western in character. Like the fifth-century Pope, Chesterton emphasises a symmetry or equality of the natures in their constitution of the incarnate Word. Chesterton's Christology remains, as we shall see, genuinely Chalcedonian — it never develops Nestorian tendencies — but it looks for the subsequent unfolding of the teaching of the Fourth Ecumenical Council to the iconography and hymnography, devotion and sensibility, of the mediaeval and post-mediaeval West. In matters of Christological orthodoxy, Chesterton has little sympathy with the Byzantine version. Unlike the present writer, he prefers Raphael to the art of the icon.

Chesterton's attitude toward Monophysitism is key here, because Monophysitism is the pressing of the orthodox doctrine of

---

[364]*Christendom in Dublin*, 86-87.

Cyril of Alexandria, as dogmatised at the Third Ecumenical Council, Ephesus, in 431, in the direction of an anti-Leonine interpretation of Chalcedon. As important historical background — not given by Chesterton and perhaps unknown to him — we can mention how the desire of the Byzantine emperors to exclude any version of Chalcedon that might give succour to Nestorianism dominated their Church policy in the sixth and seventh centuries. That desire both reflected and engendered some sympathy with the Monophysites, until in the figure of St. Maximus the Confessor the controversy over Monothelitism — the claim that there is in the incarnate Word only one will — gave the emperors pause. With the Sixth Ecumenical Council, in 681, Constantinople III, the pendulum took another swing, this time to re-emphasise the reality of the Saviour's human faculties.

Chesterton understood Monophysitism in terms of the antithesis it presents — and this is true enough — to our contemporary theological liberalism. Ancient Monophysitism was, he wrote, the "very opposite" of early-twentieth-century Modernism: "Whereas the most recent heretics are humanitarians, and would simplify the God-man by saying He was only Man, the most ancient heretics simplified Him by saying He was only God."[365] Chesterton is right if he understands by "saying He was only God" the denial that, after the union of natures at the Incarnation, the humanity of the Lord retains its own consistency, its own capacity to function according to those principles which the "man assumed" shared with the rest of the human species. Contrary to Monophysite claims, Christ was not only consubstantial with the Father; he was and is consubstantial with ourselves also. The popular Monophysite picture of Christ (we are not thinking here of such subtle and responsible

---

[365]*Christendom in Dublin*, 87.

theologians as the great Severus of Antioch) has been described as "God looking out through the eyes of a man." But Chesterton goes further and imagines the incarnate God of Monophysite devotion as looking out through the eyes, rather, of a ghost. Is this Monophysitism? Or is it really Docetism that Chesterton is speaking of? The question is unavoidable when we read such a passage as the following:

> [T]hese mystics had in their hearts the same horror as the Moslems: the horror of God abasing himself by becoming human. They were, so to speak, the anti-humanitarians. They were willing to believe that a god had somehow shown himself to the world like a ghost; but not that he had been made out of the mere mud of the world like a man.[366]

Chesterton has been arguing that Palestine-Israel, the "scene of the Incarnation," became in the aftermath of the Resurrection, "almost sealed and consecrated to the denial of the Incarnation."[367] Chesterton speaks fairly enough of the Jews of the Land whose "high monotheism eventually hardened and narrowed into a violent refusal of the Incarnation."[368] There is also truth in his claim that, under the eventual Islamic dominion, the Land was ruled by a people who "also interpreted monotheism mainly as the denial of the Incarnation; even after the Incarnation."[369]

But he does not stop there, since he wishes to argue that Monophysite Christianity exemplifies what he calls "mystical developments, tending in the same direction and thriving especially

[366] Ibid.
[367] Ibid., 86.
[368] Ibid.
[369] Ibid.

in the same neighbourhood."[370] Nor does he regard the mainstream Byzantine tradition (which never ceased to be Chalcedonian) as entirely exempt from this condition. The East Roman
rule which separates, chronologically, Jewish and pagan Roman
dominance in Judaea from Islamic, is tarred — up to a point —
with the same brush. Those who lived closest to the natural sur-
roundings of Jesus were least able to grasp how far God had
stooped down to become co-natural with them. As Chesterton
writes:

> And above all, for this is the point of the paradox, the
> Catholic Church proclaimed that original humanity more
> and more loudly, as it passed away from its original human
> habitation. As the Church marched westward she bore
> with her, with ever-increasing exultation and certitude, the
> human corporeal thing that had been made flesh in Bethle-
> hem; and left behind a ghost for the Gnostics and a god like
> a gilded idol for the Greek heretics, and for the Moslems
> only the fading shadow of a prophet.[371]

I said that Chesterton tarred the Byzantines with that same
brush with which he was painting black the Monophysites "up to a
point" because he is careful not to describe Eastern Orthodoxy as
actually heterodox in matters Christological: he distinguishes between "the truth itself" — meaning the truth of the reality of the
humanity assumed — and "the emphasis on this truth," the way
Orientals presented the truth of the reality. It was the "emphasis
on this truth, if not the truth itself" that "actually grew stronger as
the Church marched westward, from Antioch to Rome and from

---

[370]*Christendom in Dublin*, 86.
[371]Ibid., 89.

Rome to the ends of the earth."[372] Or in an alternative formulation, likewise intended to save the Christological orthodoxy of the Chalcedonian East while simultaneously indicating there was something slightly half-hearted about it: Byzantine theologians "defended rather than described the Humanity." It was Western Christendom that "made the first portraits, if not the first pictures of Christ."[373]

> The Higher Critics took a frigid pleasure in referring to their human Christ only as Jesus of Nazareth; but they could not find Him in Nazareth. They could find little or nothing in Nazareth or twenty other holy places of the East, but the flattened faces of the Greek icons or the faceless ornament of the Moslem script. Insofar as He was remembered, or at least insofar as He was imagined, as a human personality and a Man moving among men, He was seen as moving as in a hundred pictures, under Italian skies or against Flemish landscapes, a new Incarnation in colour and clay and pigments; which did not take place till He reached the coloured regions of the sunset . . .[374]

by which Chesterton means the Western Europe of Florence or Bruges.

> There are even [writes Chesterton] some dark and fearful Christs, in the more sinister phases of Byzantine art, which really look Monophysite to the point of monstrosity; and we almost look to see a wheel of six arms, holding hammers and thunderbolts . . . There was something symbolic, like a

[372] Ibid.
[373] Ibid., 91.
[374] Ibid., 90.

mysterious repetition of the Flight into Egypt, in the way in which the Mother, carrying the Divine Humanity in her arms, took refuge in the Roman world of the West; and seemed still to be fulfilling some destiny even in moving continually westward. It was as if, in some fairy tale about sunset and the islands of the blest, there was to be discovered somewhere a softer air or a more quiet light, in which the God could most freely show Himself as a Man; taking on an intimate and domestic character forgotten in the heat and the hard abstract feuds of the fiery places of his birth.[375]

It was, then, so Chesterton maintains, "Western art, Western legends, Western customs of Christmas or Easter" that "gradually unfolded the fullness of the Manhood, with which dwelt the fullness of the Godhead bodily."[376]

A Theology of the Atonement

The incorporation of that phrase from the letter to the Colossians about the divine *pleroma* subsisting bodily in Jesus informs us that Chesterton is not setting out to displace emphasis on the Godhead of Jesus by this encomium on Western devotion to the sacred humanity. As we shall see when we turn now to the topic of the Atonement, he is capable, when he thinks it rhetorically necessary, of doctrinal statements that are highly asymmetric in their stress on the divinity of Christ — even to the point of suggesting that same Monophysitism he so excoriated in *Christendom in Dublin*.

Did, then, Chesterton have a theology of the Atonement? Certainly, but for much of the time it has to be assembled from

[375]*Christendom in Dublin*, 92-93.
[376]Ibid., 93.

allusions and asides. Its character can already be discerned from Chesterton's *William Blake*. Blake, whose Christianity was jumbled up with Gnosticism, considered it a mistake on the part of the Redeemer that he so weakly accepted death. If Jesus attained in his growth to maturity the divine life, he should likewise have attained immortal life, not surrendered life on the Cross. So thought Blake, but not, however, Chesterton, who comments:

> The spectacle of a God dying is much more grandiose than the spectacle of a man living for ever. The former suggests that awful changes have really entered the alchemy of the universe; the latter is only vaguely reminiscent of hygienic octogenarians and Eno's Fruit Salts.[377]

"The spectacle of a God dying" is a striking phrase. How should we assess it? It is, of course, true that for the emerging Christology of the great Councils of the first seven centuries, the patristic era, "one of the Holy Trinity was crucified for us." That statement, originally devised in the hope of capturing Monophysite sympathies, is no capitulation to those sympathies. Rather, it captures the full implications for the death of Jesus of the clarification issued by the Fifth Ecumenical Council, Constantinople II, in 552, when it sought to tighten the formulation offered at its processor, the Fourth Council, Chalcedon, in 451. The "person" in Christ is the uncreated Word: this is he who died on the Cross.

Chalcedonianism accepts, nonetheless, that the Word existed in his two natures, including full humanity, which licenses us in speaking also, therefore, of the *man* who died — and indeed God could only die as man, in his human embodiment.

[377] *William Blake*, 179.

The highly Alexandrian, or at any rate Byzantine, statement of the Atonement Chesterton makes in *William Blake* needed to be complemented, therefore, by an account which does fuller justice to the humanity of the one who suffered.

This we can find in, for example, *Four Faultless Felons*, a novel from Chesterton's late period. In one episode, the son of an exploitative industrialist takes on the role of a criminal, breaking into people's houses or putting his hand in their pockets, in order to leave jewels and money there to compensate for his father's reduction of others to poverty.

> Don't you understand [asks this character, Alan Nadoway], how shallow all these moderns are, when they tell you there is no such thing as Atonement or Expiation, when that is the one thing for which the whole heart is sick before the sins of the world? The whole universe was wrong, while the lie of my father flourished like the green bay-tree. It was not respectability that could redeem it. It was religion, expiation, sacrificial suffering. Somebody must be terribly good, to balance what was so bad. Somebody must be *needlessly* good, to weigh down the scales of that judgment.[378]

Here Nadoway stands in the shadow, not darkening but illuminating, of the Man on the Cross. Chesterton is providing his own answer to St. Anselm's question, *Cur Deus homo?*: Why did God become man?

It was to expiate human evil by an act so utterly superfluous in the unnecessarily superabundant character of its overfulfilment of the demands of justice that the mercy it expressed redeemed the world, righted the balance. So spendthrift was God in his investment in human nature.

---

[378]*Four Faultless Felons* (London, [1930] 1936), 229.

A Christocentric Theology of History

Chesterton's fullest response to the Anselmian query is furnished, however, by the Christocentric theology of history he offers in *The Everlasting Man*. Indeed, this theology of history can be called the principal locus for his Christological contribution. We saw in the last chapter, on the image of God in man, how strongly Chesterton insists on the revolutionary — rather than merely evolutionary — character of the emergence of man from the animal realm. Chesterton orients his succeeding story towards the Incarnation by an unusual route: the significance, as he sees it, of the *structure of the family*.

In the first place, the human family reinforces the sense of the difference which separates man from other living creatures. As Chesterton puts it: "Round the family do indeed gather the sanctities that separate men from ants and bees."[379] Throughout the history of human culture, so Chesterton claims, the family retains its place and role. As he remarks elsewhere, in an essay on "The Drift from Domesticity" included in *The Thing*:

> The existing and general system of society, subject in our own age and individual culture to very great abuses and painful problems, is nevertheless a normal one. It is the idea that the commonwealth is made up of a number of small kingdoms, of which a man and a woman become the king and the queen and in which they exercise a reasonable authority, subject to the common sense of the commonwealth, until those under their care grow up to found similar kingdoms and exercise similar authority. This is the social structure of mankind, far older than all its records and more universal

[379]*The Everlasting Man*, 54.

than any of its religions; and all attempts to alter it are mere talk and tomfoolery.[380]

That "triangle," as The Everlasting Man has it, is "repeated everywhere in the pattern of the world."[381] And so we should not be surprised if the event of the Incarnation, termed by Chesterton "the highest event in history, to which all history looks forward and leads up," turns out to be what he calls "something that is at once the reversal and the renewal of that triangle."[382] A new triangle — the Holy Family: child, mother, and father — so imposed on the old triangle — father, mother, and child — as to intersect it. The effect is at once preservation and inversion: "It is in no way altered except in being entirely reversed; just as the world which was transformed was not in the least different, except in being turned upside down."[383]

In dealing with the passage of time between the moment of the emergence of humankind and the moment of the Incarnation, Chesterton is chiefly concerned to subvert the notion that this passage of time is principally a passage from barbarism to civilization. That is partly because he found some especially ancient civilizations especially impressive and so saw no reason why civil elements could not have attached to earliest man. But mainly it is because he seeks to eradicate the habit of mind for which "at every stage" barbarism is something to which we "look back," civilization something to which we "look forward."[384] That version of historical determinism would discourage us, even if it did not

[380]The Thing, 40.
[381]The Everlasting Man, 55.
[382]Ibid.
[383]Ibid.
[384]Ibid., 71.

entirely disable us, from considering certain episodes in the Roman Palestine of the first decades of the Common Era to be the real climax of history. But, as we know, they were.

The key to the Incarnation as the climax of history is, for Chesterton, the realization that, in his words, "Man could do no more."[385] On Chesterton's interpretation of the movement of human history — in, not exclusively but mainly, what was for him its central theatre, the Mediterranean basin — the two chief impulses which lead human beings to conceive the overall purpose of the world — the mythopoeic impulse which generates mythology and the rational impulse which produces philosophy — had exhausted their resources for doing just that in any fully coherent and satisfying way. In this crucial test-case, human capacities had been shown to have run up against their limit.

Chesterton's argument is complex but cumulative. While recognising the heterogeneity of religions, he treats the use of the mythopoeic mode as the essence of paganism. "The power even in the myths of savages is like the power in the metaphors of poets . . . it is an attempt to reach the divine reality through the imagination alone."[386] In pagan culture (he means outside the Abrahamic faiths) the religious imagination works both negatively and positively.

Negatively, by various indicators — ranging from references to a high God who has withdrawn to the vague etherialising of the divine represented by the Chinese term "Heaven" — the religious imagination signals its sense of the "presence of the absence of God."[387] This absence, whether in polytheism or in agnosticism, was serious stuff.

---

[385] *The Everlasting Man,* 210.
[386] Ibid., 105, 110.
[387] Ibid., 93.

[T]he world would have been lost if it had been unable to return to that great original simplicity of a single authority in all things . . . that we live in a large and serene world under a sky that stretches paternally over all the peoples of the earth . . .[388]

It was, for Chesterton, the unique vocation of Israel — she who is by definition outside the nations, the *goyim* — to keep that conviction alive, if only, for the time being, on a "tribal" foundation.

Positively, however, through paganism in the mythopoeic mode there runs the "love of locality and personality." There was, feels Chesterton, "a truth in it that could not be left out, though it were a lighter and less essential truth."[389] "[H]e who has no sympathy with myths has no sympathy with men."[390] Pagan religion in that mode satisfied the need for "the twin ideas of festivity and formality."[391] By its sacrificial cultus it also partly satisfied the human need to "surrender . . . something as the portion of the unknown powers."[392] Most importantly, however, it expressed the "indestructible instinct, in the poet as represented by the pagan, that he is not entirely wrong in localising his God."[393] But since the "laws and triumphs" of imagination are not necessarily reality-related, the way of mythology could only be

a *search*: it is something that combines a recurrent desire with a recurrent doubt, mixing a most hungry sincerity in the

---

[388]*The Everlasting Man*, 97-98.

[389]Ibid., 99.

[390]Ibid., 109.

[391]Ibid.

[392]Ibid., 111.

[393]Ibid., 113.

idea of seeking for a place with a most dark and deep and mysterious levity about all the places found.[394]

The gods have a "great deal of nonsense about them": often it is "good nonsense," though sometimes (Chesterton has especially the religions of tropical America in mind, as well as ancient Carthage[395]) it may be demonic.[396]

Chesterton draws a very sharp contrast between mythopoeic religion and philosophical rationality: "It is vital to the view of all history that reason is something separate from religion even in the most rational of these civilisations."[397] Merely by an "afterthought" do a "few Neo-Platonists or a few Brahmins" try to rationalise the gods — generally by allegorisation.[398] "But in reality the rivers of mythology and philosophy run parallel and do not mingle till they meet in the sea of Christendom."[399] Ambitiously, Chesterton runs through the philosophers of ancient Greece and what he terms the "royal philosophers" — whether princes or the advisers to princes — of China (Confucius), Egypt (the pharaoh Akhenaton), and India (Gautama, the Buddha), as well as the "sages" of Persia (Manes, Zoroaster). His criticism of them all is *false simplification*: "They all think that existence can be represented by a diagram instead of a drawing, and the rude drawings of the childish

[394] Ibid.

[395] The key to Chesterton's exaltation of the Roman Republic and Empire is that, in her final unexpected victory over Carthage with its dreadful religion, "all men knew in their hearts that she had been representative of mankind, even when she was rejected of men" (ibid., 150).

[396] Ibid., 118.

[397] Ibid., 110-111.

[398] Ibid., 111.

[399] Ibid.

myth-makers are a sort of crude and spirited protest against that view."[400] But in late antiquity, mythology, which, since it was "never thought" could not be revived and thus sustained,[401] became increasingly trivial, while the philosophers, who had never succeeded in generating consensus, tended to degenerate into "hired rhetoricians."[402]

In this situation, when "Man could do no more," the preaching of the gospel was "as if a new meteoric metal had fallen on the earth; it was a difference of substance to the touch. Those who touched their foundation fancied they had struck a rock."[403] In the cave of Bethlehem, it was a "hole in the rocks" which "marked the position of one outcast and homeless . . . [T]he God who had been only a circumference was seen as a centre, and a centre is infinitely small.[404] In the "riddle of Bethlehem," "heaven was under the earth." It is easy to see where Chesterton is heading. The *philosophical* affirmation of pure deity in its almighty relationship with everything that is not divine is here combined with the *mythopoeic* celebration of a little child: "The populace had been wrong in many things; but they had not been wrong in believing that holy things could have a habitation and that divinity need not disdain the limits of time and space."[405] Since that hour of Christ's birth, writes Chesterton, doubtless somewhat sweepingly, "no mythologies have been made in the world. Mythology is a search."[406] What,

---

[400] *The Everlasting Man*, 136.

[401] Ibid., 160.

[402] Ibid., 161.

[403] Ibid., 164.

[404] Ibid., 173, 172. The title "the divine Outcast" for Jesus Christ had been much favoured in Noel's Thaxted.

[405] Ibid., 174.

[406] Ibid., 175.

then, of philosophy? At the manger-cave its terms are changed, as the visit of the Magi, the representatives of philosophical wisdom, should tell us.

Philosophy also, like mythology, had very much the air of a search. It is the realisation of this truth that gives its traditional majesty and mystery to the figures of the Three Kings; the discovery that religion is broader than philosophy, and that this is the broadest of religions, contained within this narrow space.[407]

Under the heading "the riddles of the Gospel," Chesterton will go on to evoke the enigmatic mode of teaching of the adult Jesus which

if anyone says it is what might be expected of a man walking about in that place at that period, we can quite fairly answer that it is much *more* like what might be the mysterious utterance of a being beyond man, if he walked alive among men.[408]

He will also resume for us the "strangest story in the world": "a romance of the pursuit of the ultimate sacrifice," such that

from the moment when the star goes up like a birthday rocket to the moment when the sun is extinguished like a funeral torch, the whole story moves on wings with the speed and direction of a drama, ending with an act beyond words.[409]

---

[407] Ibid., 179.
[408] Ibid., 196.
[409] *The Everlasting Man*, 207.

G. K. Chesterton, Theologian

On Good Friday, all three of Rome, Jerusalem, and Athens were present and where the "best things in the world" were "at their worst" we are shown "the world at its worst."[410] But where men could do no more, God acted supremely. At Easter, the disciples "in varying ways realised the new wonder" — but "even they did not realise that the world had died in the night." What they were looking at was "the first day of a new creation."[411]

Yet I do not think we find any more sublime, or for that matter quintessentially Chestertonian, statement than his comment on the cave of Bethlehem:

> [I]t is the paradox of that group in the cave, that while our emotions about it are of childish simplicity, our thoughts about it can branch with a never-ending complexity. And we can never reach the end even of our own ideas about the child who was a father and the mother who was a child.[412]

The closing words of that citation, let it be said, breathe the atmosphere of Chesterton's tender devotion to Mary the Mother of God, of which so many of his poems — most notably those contained in *The Queen of Seven Swords* — are filled.[413]

Conclusion

In *The Everlasting Man* Chesterton pursues the fundamental idea of a Christological reconciliation of mythology and philosophy very consistently to the end. I find it impossible not to insert

---

[410]*The Everlasting Man*, 210.

[411]Ibid., 213.

[412]Ibid.

[413]*The Queen of Seven Swords* (London, 1926).

a reference here to the theological aesthetics of Hans Urs von Balthasar, in which the gap between the mythopoeic and the philosophical is unbridgeable without the Incarnation. Myth and philosophy are like

> a bridge which is being thrown out from two piers on opposite shores and which seems all the time to be approaching the point where both constructions meet, yet always remains intrinsically incapable of being completed.[414]

For Chesterton, the faith which sprang from the event of Jesus Christ *is* "the reconciliation" — in Balthasar's term, the "bridge" — precisely because it is the "realization both of mythology and philosophy."[415]

> It is a story, and in that sense one of a hundred stories; only it is a true story. It is a philosophy, and in that sense one of a hundred philosophies; only it is like life. But above all it is a reconciliation that can only be called the philosophy of stories. That normal narrative instinct which produced all the fairy tales was neglected by all the philosophies — except one. The Faith is the justification of that popular instinct; the finding of the philosophy for it or the analysis of the philosophy in it.[416]

---

[414]H. U. von Balthasar, *The Glory of the Lord: A Theological Aesthetics. IV. The Realm of Metaphysics in Antiquity* (Edinburgh, 1989), 216.

[415]*The Everlasting Man,* 246.

[416]Ibid. We can note that Chesterton does not make the mistake of supposing that a "narrative theology" can stand alone, without some philosophical integument, accompaniment, or exploration. See F. A. Murphy, *God Is Not a Story: Realism Revisited* (Oxford, 2007).

And Chesterton looks back for a moment (this, at any rate, is my surmise) to the world of *Heretics* which he had left behind, and that of *Orthodoxy* which he still inhabited, when he concludes of non-Christian philosophies:

> Each of them starves the story-telling instinct, so to speak, and does something to spoil human life considered as a romance; either by fatalism (pessimist or optimist) and the destiny that is the death of adventure; or by indifference and that detachment that is the death of drama; or by a fundamental scepticism that dissolves the actors into atoms; or by a materialistic limitation blocking the vista of moral consequences; or by a mechanical recurrence making even moral tests monotonous; or a bottomless relativity making even practical texts insecure.[417]

In this human story that is also a divine story the mythological search for romance and the philosophical search for truth were alike fulfilled, in a figure who was both historical and ideal.

> The more deeply we think of the matter, the more we shall conclude that, if indeed there be a God, his creation could hardly have reached any other culmination than this granting of a real romance to the world.[418]

Otherwise, the human creature would have remained ineluctably schizophrenic, one lobe of the brain "dreaming impossible dreams" and the other "repeating invariable calculations." It was "this abyss that nothing but an incarnation could cover."[419] The

---

[417] *The Everlasting Man*, 246.
[418] Ibid., 248.
[419] Ibid.

"true story of the world" could be given only by revelation from above, since a story is always told by one to another, and who could this "one" be but God if the "other" were the world? But once it was told, the story could restore the sanity of the world and offer the soul salvation.

Chapter 8

Chesterton as Theological Ethicist

In *Chesterton and the Edwardian Cultural Crisis* John Coates singles out with peculiar emphasis Chesterton's identification of a "latent irrationalism" among his contemporaries, owing to their lack of any pondered theory of the good.[420] Chesterton was well aware of the importance of the cultural domain. He wrote in *Fancies Versus Fads*: "Man, as Aristotle saw long ago, is an abnormal animal whose nature it is to be civilized. Insofar as he ever becomes uncivilized he becomes unnatural, and even artificial."[421] Chesterton realised, however, that culture cannot flourish unless it is underpinned by the virtues. In their interrelated functioning, the virtues are constitutive of the human good. Authentic culture has a moral structure, the character of which can be thought through, in the first place, by reference to human nature itself. The moral structure of culture, in other words, is not without its own preconditions in ontology — in the discovery of what reality, and notably *our* reality,

---

[420]I make use in this chapter of some material previously published under the title "G. K. Chesterton as Moralist of Culture" in A. Nichols, O.P., *Beyond the Blue Glass: Catholic Essays on Faith and Culture* (London, 2002), 65-80.

[421]*Fancies Versus Fads*, 182.

is like. Orage, the editor of the progressive Edwardian journal *The New Age*, appears to have been converted from his Nietzschean view of man-in-constant-evolution-towards-Superman by acceptance of Chesterton's thesis that much of the crisis of modernity stems from an unwillingness to recognise the *definiteness* of the human species, and consequently the definiteness likewise of our nature's native good. As Orage put it, in words that might have been written by Chesterton himself:

> Starting from a false conception of the nature of man, the mind continually sees everything in a false light. Its whole object is to become something that it really is not, and can never be . . . with human nature undefined, nothing else is definable.[422]

The criterion for determining what human dispositions really are moral virtues, or habits vitally necessary to the flourishing of man in culture, is, then, human nature. But that does not necessarily mean human nature *humanistically conceived*.

Ethics and the Supernatural

There are two reasons for adding that important qualification. In the first place, our grasp of the first principles of reasoning about human nature, and the virtues which belong to its perfection, may be, naturally speaking, uncertain. We are living, after all, in a post-lapsarian age, after the Fall of Adam. Our grasp on the relevant principles may need steadying, then, supernaturally — that is, by divine revelation. In *Orthodoxy* Chesterton was evidently aware of this problem: people can be really quite lunatic in

---

[422]Cited in W. Martin, *The "New Age" Under Orage* (London, 1967), 215.

their attempts at rational judgment of the good for man. As he wrote:

> The chief mark and element of insanity is reason used without root, reason in the void. The man who begins to think without the proper first principles goes mad, the man who begins to think at the wrong end.[423]

So revelation may be needed in order to confirm which principles really are the primary principles of reason in evaluating human nature and its moral needs. *Orthodoxy* belongs, of course, to Chesterton's Anglo-Catholic period, but it would not be difficult to show that it reflects — no doubt unwittingly — this insistence of the [Roman] Catholic magisterial tradition, notably articulated at the First Vatican Council of 1869-1870. Strictly speaking, so that council explained, human reason is able by its own natural power and light to attain a true and certain knowledge of the natural law written by the Creator in human hearts. But *de facto* the human mind is hampered in the attaining of such truths, not least by the disorder in our appetites which follows on Original Sin. In moral matters, people easily persuade themselves that what it does not suit them to hold as true is actually false or at best doubtful. So divine revelation has a key part to play in facilitating humanity's grasp of the natural moral order.[424]

The second reason for saying that the criterion of the moral good is human nature but not human nature "humanistically conceived" turns on a very different question, and that is the supernatural — the more-than-natural — "finality" (goal, orientation,

---

[423]*Orthodoxy*, 30.

[424]Cf. *Dei Filius* (the dogmatic constitution of the First Vatican Council on faith and reason), 2.

direction), which, according to Scripture, God wills for our human nature in his plan to transfigure and consummate it in his beloved Son. In the concrete divine economy of creation and salvation, our human nature is ordered towards a superhuman goal. As Chesterton wrote in *The Thing*:

> For Catholics it is a fundamental dogma of the Faith that all human beings, without any exception whatever, are specially made, were specially shaped and pointed like shining arrows, for the end of hitting the mark of Beatitude . . .[425]

the super-fulfilment of which is sharing in the life of the divine Trinity by seeing the Father through the Son in the Holy Spirit. That supernatural finality does not mean, however, that human nature ceases to exist as a natural reality when it enters the order of grace. It means, rather, that the good of that nature can now be achieved only *by way of* the supernatural. Some features of the good for man can, therefore, be identified — in principle, not merely in practice — only by means of divine revelation, in a superhuman, more-than-human, way. There are, accordingly, moral virtues key to human flourishing in the context of grace that were unknown, or at best barely surmised, outside the sphere of revelation — for instance, charity, the virtue that bids us love our neighbour for God's sake that he may be in God: what Jesus himself called, in his Last Supper discourse, the "new commandment."

On both grounds — the practical difficulty of persuading people of the basic truth of natural ethics without the supplementary confirmation of revelation, and the theoretical impossibility, or near-impossibility, of establishing the higher norms of supernatural ethics without the historic revelation which comes to its

---

[425]*The Thing*, 26.

climax in Jesus Christ — appeal to the Gospel as a fount of doctrine on not only faith but also morals is required. And therefore appeal to the Church is required, since the Church is responsible for Gospel transmission. As Chesterton put it in *The Thing* (again):

> [H]ere humanism cannot substitute for super-Humanism. The modern world, with its modern movement, is living on Catholic capital. It is using, and using up, the truths that remain to it out of the old treasury of Christendom, including of course many truths known to pagan antiquity but crystallised in Christendom.[426]

The Pattern of the Virtues

Many twentieth-century Christian writers would no doubt have said the same thing. What is distinctive about Chesterton is the emphasis he lays on the holistic pattern of the virtues in their interrelations, the total picture which they represent. There are not only particular virtues, natural or supernatural, which we need. There is also an overall configuration of the virtues which we need. *En route* to its beatitude our determinate human nature cannot flourish without doing so in and through a definite constellation of good dispositions. The virtues do not just sit next to each other in a catalogue. They belong with each other in a pattern, an ordered totality. They make up a significant form, and it is this form which disintegrates outside of faith and which humanism, try as it will, is powerless to re-integrate. It cannot put Humpty-Dumpty together again. Citing one last time from *The Thing*:

[426]Ibid., 22.

> Humanism may try to pick up the pieces; but can it stick
> them together? . . . What is to prevent one Humanist want-
> ing chastity without humility, and another humility with-
> out chastity, and another truth or beauty without either?
> The problem of an enduring ethic and culture consists in
> finding an arrangement of the pieces by which they re-
> main related, as do the stones arranged in an arch. And I
> know only one scheme that has thus proved its solidity,
> bestriding lands and age with its gigantic arches and carry-
> ing everywhere the high river of baptism upon an aqueduct
> of Rome.[427]

While something along those lines might have come from
Chesterton's pen in the period opened by the writing of *Orthodoxy*, in fact *The Thing* dates from 1929, when Chesterton has left
Anglo-Catholicism behind and discovered with Petrine communion the thought of St Thomas Aquinas. In Thomas's ethics the
idea of the unity of the virtues plays an important part. It is a notion
which has made a remarkable comeback in some more recent, late-
twentieth-century, ethics, in a way which would have gladdened
Chesterton's heart. In *After Virtue*, written in 1981, Alasdair Mac-
Intyre had repudiated the notion that, in his words, "there exists a
cosmic order which dictates the place of each virtue in a total
harmonious scheme of human life," such that moral truth consists in moral judgment conforming to this scheme. But so varied
and heterogeneous are human goods that "their pursuit cannot
be reconciled in any single moral order." To attempt that is to risk
enfolding the human condition in a "totalitarian straitjacket."
That goes for "heterogeneity of the virtues" as well as goods in

---

[427] *The Thing*, 34.

general.[428] Seven years later, he changed his mind completely. [429] In a successor volume, *Whose Justice, Which Rationality?*, he declared, "The unity of the virtues is exhibited in what is required to perfect each of them."[430]

It would not be misleading to say that throughout his life Chesterton was seeking how best that mutual perfecting of the virtues could take place, and, correspondingly, what was the best way to express the moral structure needed for culture — though no doubt he would have spurned the word "structure" as excessively geometric, not to say jejune. In *Orthodoxy* he calls what I have termed a "structure" "an exact and perilous balance, like that of a desperate romance." In another formulation he speaks of it as no

> mere victory of some one thing swallowing up everything
> else, love, or pride or peace or adventure; [instead] it must
> be a definite picture composed of those elements in their
> best proportion and relation.[431]

Perhaps the most striking statement of this Chestertonian project of pointing up the human good as a structured whole comes in Chesterton's discussion of the mediaeval English poet Geoffrey Chaucer. In his *Chaucer: A Study* he takes up the idea of a harmonious equilibrium and works it into a more mobile and flowing simile, the simile of the "dance" of the virtues. What Chesterton adds here to his account in *Orthodoxy* is above all an explicitly

---

[428] A. MacIntyre, *After Virtue: A Study in Moral Theory* (London, 1985, second edition), 142, 143.

[429] Idem., *Whose Justice, Which Rationality?* (London, 1988), x.

[430] Ibid., p. 198. For his change of position, see C. S. Lutz, *Tradition in the Ethics of Alasdair MacIntyre: Relativism, Thomism and Philosophy* (Lanham, Maryland, 2004), 101-104.

[431] *Orthodoxy*, 166.

Christological dimension. The dance of the virtues has for its centre a unique still point in the turning world, and this is the disclosure of the ultimately Christological character of the human good, with Christ as the true midpoint, then, of culture. To convey this vision Chesterton makes use of the well-known English nursery rhyme, "Here We Go Round the Mulberry Bush." He writes:

> Medieval morality was full of the idea that one thing must balance another, that each stood on one side or the other of something that was in the middle, and something remained in the middle.There might be any amount of movement, but it was movement round this central thing; perpetually altering the attitudes, but preserving the balance. The virtues were like children going round the Mulberry Bush, only the Mulberry Bush was that Burning Bush which they made symbolical of the Incarnation; that flamboyant bush in which the Virgin and Child appear in the picture . . .

In mediaeval iconography the Burning Bush is normally an *emblem* of the Incarnation, not a full pictorial representation, and so Chesterton signals to us he has a definite painting in mind. It is in fact Nicolas Froment's late-fifteenth-century triptych *The Burning Bush* in the cathedral of *Saint-Sauveur* at Aix-en-Provence. There indeed, to revert to the text of *Chaucer*:

> the Virgin and Child appear in the picture, with René of Provence and his beloved wife kneeling at their side. Now [Chesterton goes on] since that break in history, whatever we call it or whatever we think of it [the ending, he means, of the mediaeval world], the Dance has turned into a Race. That is, the dancers lose their balance and only recover it by running towards some object, or alleged object;

not an object within their circle or their possession, but an object which they do not yet possess. It is a flying object, a disappearing object.

Chesterton insists he is not at the moment concerned with "condemning or commending the religion of the Race or the religion of the Dance." He insists:

> I am only pointing out that this is the fundamental difference between them. One is rhythmic and recurrent movement, because there is a known centre; while the other is precipitate or progressive movement, because there is an unknown goal . . .

In contrast with the accelerated pace of modern life, "Canterbury pilgrims do not seem to be in a very great hurry to get to Canterbury."[432] The "religion of the Race" is, of course, the ideology of progress, which Chesterton, whatever his self-restraint in this passage, thought to be absurd because of its lack of either clear goal or fixed standard of value.

Among twentieth-century critics of liberal secularism and its effects in culture, then, Chesterton is distinctive in the emphasis he lays on the holistic pattern of the virtues necessary for human flourishing or human perfection. But where he seems to be more than merely distinctive — to be in fact unique — is in his account of the argument that when the pattern disintegrates, the individual virtues may do as much damage as the vices. He writes in *Orthodoxy*:

> The modern world is not evil; in some ways the modern world is far too good. It is full of wild and wasted virtues.

[432]*Chaucer: A Study* (London, 1932), 158-159.

G. K. Chesterton, Theologian

When a religious scheme is shattered (as Christianity was shattered by the Reformation), it is not merely the vices that are let loose. The vices are, indeed, let loose, and they wander and do damage. But the virtues are let loose also; and the virtues do more terrible damage. The modern world is full of the old Christian virtues gone mad. The virtues have gone mad because they have been isolated from one another and are wandering alone. Thus some scientists care for truth; and their truth is pitiless. Thus some humanitarians only care for pity; and their pity (I am sorry to say) is often untruthful.[433]

A *Pseudo-virtue: Innovativeness*

But it is time to look at what the particular virtues are that Chesterton assembles in the ring o'roses around the Supreme Good in his own incarnate form. We can notice by way of preamble how briskly Chesterton disposes of what may be the most praised virtue in our own culture, namely, innovativeness, especially of a technical or economic kind. Chesterton did not believe that the imperative, *Be technically or economically innovative*, of itself specified a range of actions belonging to a virtue. For such innovations must always be judged in terms of their congruence with human nature, with the human good. Thus, in *The Victorian Age in Literature* he observes that innovations in transport and communications are of secondary significance compared with the question, *Is what is being transported or communicated worthwhile?*

The Victorians . . . could not or would not see that humanity repels or welcomes the railway train, simply according to

[433]*Orthodoxy*, 34-35.

what people come by it. They could not see that one welcomes or smashes the telephone, according to what words
one hears in it.[434]

The innovativeness admired by an entrepreneurial culture of an
advanced technological kind can only be regarded as a pre-moral
trait until we know what good, if any, it serves in the human
scheme as a whole. The unwillingness to raise such fundamental
questions stemmed for Chesterton from the exaggerated empiricism
of an intellectual culture that had narrowed its own base without
warrant. In the course of the nineteenth century

> [t]he duty of dragging out by the tail or the hind leg or any
> other corner one can possibly get hold of [i.e., empirical en-
> quiry], a perfectly sound duty in itself, had somehow come
> into collision with the older and larger duty of knowing
> something about the organism and ends of a creature; or, in
> the everyday phrase, being able to make head or tail of it.[435]

There can be no wisdom without the willingness to put the
"why" question, to seek to know the causes of things — both in
terms of final causality, by understanding the purpose of human
living, and in terms of formal causality, by understanding the kind
of things human beings are.

Archaiophilia

If we now leave a pseudo-virtue for the real thing, we find
Chesterton commending a wonderful range of virtues in the
course of his work. I begin with one of the more controversial of

---

[434]*The Victorian Age in Literature*, 211.
[435]Ibid.

his circle of virtues, not because it is in any way pre-eminent there, but simply on the grounds that he considered its practice a necessary condition for gaining the large view of the human creature without which all informational knowledge will fail to add up to wisdom. I call this first virtue (which has no ancient or mediaeval name, a fact that rather underlines the peculiar juncture humanity reached in the modern era) "archaiophilia" — literally "love of the past." By archaiophilia we love the past not because it is past — that would be mere historical nostalgia — but because it furnishes contemporary culture (this anyway was Chesterton's conviction) with myriad illuminating exemplars of the human good. The word *archaios* means in Greek not only that which is ancient but also that which is connected with abiding principles. In *What's Wrong with the World* Chesterton opined:

> The future is a blank wall on which every man can write his own name as large as he likes; the past [he added ironically] I find already covered with illegible scribbles, such as Plato, Isaiah, Shakespeare, Michelangelo, Napoleon.[436]

Nor is this a question simply of learning from outstanding individuals. Where modern education eliminates historical retrospection as a guide to life, it cuts off from our gaze the equally instructive life-ways of the silent masses of mankind who lived before us. In *Orthodoxy* Chesterton defined tradition as "democracy extended through time."

> Tradition means giving votes to the most obscure of all classes, our ancestors. It is the democracy of the dead. Tradition refuses to submit to the small and arrogant oligarchy of

---

[436]*What's Wrong with the World* (London, 1913), 27.

those who merely happen to be walking about. All demo-crats object to men being disqualified by the accident of birth; tradition objects to their being disqualified by the accident of death.[437]

Fraternity (and Justice)

Archaiophilia readily introduces us, then, to the practice of another virtue, fraternity. An excessive sensitivity to human difference — to the differences between individuals and groups — is endemic in our contemporary cultural radicalism. Chesterton discussed the same phenomenon in the context of the psychological novel and the class distinctions in the capitalist society of his day. Overemphasis on difference, he thought, militates against the human essence and undermines fraternity, the bonds which we should create or sustain because we belong with each other in the same species. Too much celebration of diversity works against the unity of the human race, which, seen theologically, is not only a truth found in revelation, from Genesis onward, but also a presupposition of the universal mission of the Church. In *The Victorian Age in Literature* Chesterton reminds his readers of the gamut of Chaucerian characters that made their way to the shrine of the "holy blissful martyr," Thomas à Becket, and he enquires whether a similar selection of modern figures from the nineteenth-century novel could even be imagined on some similar common journey. Having assembled a collection of characters from Thackeray, strongly contrasting in their social categories and individual temperaments, Chesterton asks rhetorically, "To what sort of distant saint would [this collection] travel, laughing and telling tales together?"

[437]*Orthodoxy*, 63.

The answer, of course, is that there is none, and he draws the conclusion, "We have gained in sympathy, but we have lost in brotherhood."[438] As the invocation of Becket's shrine may suggest, Chesterton thought the virtue of fraternity could only fully be exercised in the context of what he called "positive religion."

> Man is merely man only when he is seen against the sky. If he is seen against any landscape, he is only a man of that land. If he is seen against any house, he is only a householder. Only where death and eternity are intensely present can human beings feel their fellowship.[439]

It was because the working classes, rural and urban, had retained certain features of that fundamental fellowship — Chesterton singled out their charity to neighbours, their humour, and their reverence for the dead — that he made what we can call, in the language of liberation theology, his "option for the poor." This was an option for the recovery of qualities belonging to the human patrimony as such, qualities identified by observation of the characteristic virtues of the poor — though he was not so starry-eyed as to think that all the poor exhibit these virtues at all times. From his earliest Socialist phase Chesterton had never ceased to be preoccupied by the wider condition of society, what his early Victorian predecessors would have called the "condition of England question." He considered that what he termed "oppression by oblivion" was a typical feature of English capitalism. The worker, in his combination of economic dependence and, after the third of the Parliamentary Reform acts, political independence, was easily forgotten because, unlike a slave, he was not under the eye of a

[438]*The Victorian Age in Literature*, 98.
[439]Ibid.

master, but hired and sacked according to need. The larger part of a nation could thus be neglected through absence of mind. This was an assault on a third virtue closely connected to the virtue of fraternity, and that is the virtue of justice, by which we tend to give every man his due. As Chesterton put it in his study of William Cobbett:

> [T]his negative and indirect injustice was native both to what is good and what is bad in the English temper. It is the paradox of the English that they are always being cruel through an aversion to cruelty. They dislike quite sincerely the sight of pain, and therefore shut their eyes to it; and it was not unnatural that they should prefer a system in which men were starved in slums but not scourged in slave-compounds.[440]

Domesticity

From humanity itself, Chesterton turns his attention to the smallest of human units — the family — when proposing a fourth key virtue, the virtue of domesticity. This is a virtue which is requisite for the smallest possible polity, the home. In *The Superstition of Divorce* Chesterton called the family "the small state founded on the sexes [which] is at once the most voluntary and the most natural of all self-governing states."

Chesterton then draws on W. S. Gilbert's comic song from the Savoy opera *H.M.S. Pinafore* where the chorus reflect that the Captain of the *Pinafore* who "himself has said it/ And it's greatly to his credit,/ That he is an Englishman": might in other circumstances "have been a Roosian,/ A French, or Turk, or Proosian":

---

[440]*William Cobbett*, 222.

"It is not true of Mr Brown that he might have been a Russian, but it may be true of Mrs Brown that she might have been a Robinson."[441] The vow that is, then, perfectly freely made in order to establish this polity — the marriage vow — must be equally firmly kept for the reason that uniquely weighty consequences are attached to it in the form of children. Owing to its link with procreation, the marriage covenant that brings into existence this miniature yet irreplaceable polis is unlike any mere contract. "There is no contract that can bring cherubs (or goblins) to inhabit a small modern villa."[442] In his essay on marriage in *Come to Think of It* Chesterton observed that the same arguments as those used in favour of divorce could also be invoked in favour of murder.

> If it is true that we may sometimes solve a social problem by breaking a vow, it is equally true that we might often solve it by cutting a throat. If the immediate relaxation of an individual strain justifies everything, then Aunt Susan is indeed in danger, and the life of Cousin James trembles in the balance.[443]

Idiaphilia

So as to create the optimal conditions for the exercise of the virtue of domesticity, Chesterton believed another virtue had to be engaged. Like archaiophilia, already discussed, it has no name. So once again I shall invent one on Chesterton's behalf, and call it "idiaphilia," the appropriate love for personal property,

---

[441] *The Superstition of Divorce* (London, 1920), 23.

[442] Ibid.

[443] *Come to Think of It*, 9.

from the Greek *ta idia* meaning "one's own things." (Chesterton would probably have harrumphed, and declared this virtue to be, quite simply, the virtue of justice. But he saw justice in a very distinctive way.)

Idiaphilia was key to the programme of the Distributist League, originally entitled as it was "The League for the Preservation of Liberty by the Restoration of Property." The primary objects of the League, whose chairman Chesterton became, were: first, the preservation of property, so as to safeguard the liberty of the individual and family, and secondly, as a way to preserve property, the better distribution of capital through wide personal ownership of the means of production.[444]

The League supported, to cite its own propaganda:

> Small Shops and Shopkeepers against multiple shops and trusts. Individual Craftsmanship and Cooperation in industrial enterprise. (Every worker should own a share in the Assets and Control of the business in which he works.) The Small Holder and Yeoman Farmer against monopolists of large inadequately farmed estates.[445]

Such a programme was essentially intended to support the exercise of domesticity. In Chesterton's words in *The Superstition of Divorce*: "Too much capitalism does not mean too many capitalists, but too few capitalists, and so aristocracy sins, not in planting a family tree but in not planting a family forest."[446] Historically, there have been many intermediate groups between the individual and

---

[444]J. P. Corrin, *G. K. Chesterton and Hilaire Belloc: The Battle Against Modernity*, 108-109.

[445]Cited in ibid., 109.

[446]*The Superstition of Divorce*, 41.

the State but, writes Chesterton, "there is only one type among them which all human beings have a spontaneous and omnipresent inspiration to build for themselves; and this type is the family."[447] The family is the "only check" on the State that is "bound to renew itself as eternally as the State, and more naturally than the State."[448]

If we ask how can this be called an aspect of *theological* ethics, Chesterton's address to the first meeting of the League throws light. In *G. K.'s Weekly*, the League's journalistic mouthpiece, he and his colleagues, so he told a political meeting:

> believed in the very simple social idea that a man felt happier, more dignified, and more like the image of God, when the hat he is wearing is his own hat, and not only his hat, but his house, the ground he trod on, and various other things. There might be people who preferred to have their hats leased out to them every other week, or wear their neighbours' hats in rotation to express the idea of comradeship, or possibly to crowd under one very large hat to represent an even larger cosmic conception; but most of them felt that something was added to the dignity of men when they put on their own hats.[449]

Other Virtues That Circle Love

Other virtues which loom large in Chesterton's writing are magnanimity, chivalry, and courage, and the more especially evangelical

---

[447]*The Superstition of Divorce*, 42.

[448]Ibid., 67.

[449]Cited in W. R. Titterton, *G. K. Chesterton: A Portrait* (London, 1936), 172.

trio of simplicity, innocence, and humility.[450] Chesterton had an extraordinary vivid sense of such virtues. As he put it in *Tremendous Trifles*:

> Virtue is not the absence of vices or the avoidance of moral dangers; virtue is a vivid and separate thing, like pain or a particular smell. Mercy does not mean not being cruel or sparing people revenge or punishment; it means a plain and positive thing like the sun, which one has either seen or not seen. Chastity does not mean abstention from sexual wrong; it means something flaming, like Joan of Arc. In a word, God paints in many colours; but He never paints so gorgeously, I had almost said so gaudily, as when He paints in white.[451]

Certainly white is the liturgical colour for virgins. But Chesterton never painted so gorgeously, I think, as when he did so in scarlet.

In his study of *Chaucer* he ends by lauding the virtue of charity as what gives form to all the assembled virtues. Charity provides the mould which gives them, whether they be natural or supernatural, their true vindication and proper role. In an extraordinary visionary passage of the book Chesterton sees Chaucer, standing between the two other principal English mediaeval poets, and apparelled in this way in Jesus Christ.

---

[450] For a detection of the "family resemblance" joining Chesterton with Hans Urs von Balthasar in his account of those evangelical virtues, see J. Saward, *The Way of the Lamb: The Spirit of Childhood and the End of the Age* (Edinburgh, 1999), 123-149.

[451] *Tremendous Trifles* (London, 1909), 5-6.

Between the black robes of Gower and the grey gown of
Langland he stands clothed in scarlet like all the household
of love; and emblazoned with the Sacred Heart.[452]

The all-embracing, form-giving virtue of charity, so Chesterton
held, saturated the sensibility of Chaucer. Were we to ask Chesterton what is the evidence for that, he would reply, I think, in terms
he used elsewhere when he wrote of the early-nineteenth-century
French novelist Honoré de Balzac:

The morality of a great writer is not the morality he teaches
but the morality he takes for granted. The Catholic type of
Christian ethics runs through Balzac's books, exactly as the
Puritan type of ethics runs through Bunyan's books. What
his professed opinions were I do not know, any more than I
know Shakespeare's; but I know that both those great cre-
ators of a multitudinous world [Balzac's great series of novels
had the general title La Comédie humaine] made it, as compared with other and later writers, on the same fundamental moral plan as the universe of Dante.[453]

Chaucer, Chesterton explained:

had the one thing needful; he had the frame of mind that is
the ultimate result of right reason and a universal philosophy;
the temper that is the flower and fruit of all the tillage and the
toil of moralists and theologians. He had Charity; that is the
heart and not merely the mind of our ancient Christendom.[454]

[452]Chaucer, 75.

[453]The Superstition of Divorce, 35.

[454]Chaucer: A Study, 293. Chesterton's medievalism has been pillo-
ried, but as John Coates has written, its subtlety has not been understood: "The unjustly neglected late novel The Return of Don

In this all the virtues come together, not least the natural ones, for this was:

> the shout that showed that normality had been found. For a great voice was given by God, and a great volume of singing, not to his saints who deserved it much better . . . but only suddenly, and for a season, to the most human of human beings.[455]

Conclusion

In *Heretics* Chesterton had complained that the contemporary intelligentsia lacked the positive concept of perfection. Neither designating saints nor determining who was the "most human of human beings" (Geoffrey Chaucer can hardly be the only candidate) figured in their ethical scheme. A conversation between Father Brown and an academic who professes the Human Sciences points up the contrast. In "The Man with Two Beards," Professor Crake asks Brown, "Don't you believe that criminology is a science?" "I'm not sure," replied Father Brown. "Do you believe that hagiology is a science? . . ." And he adds: "You see, the Dark Ages tried to make a science about good people. But our own humane and enlightened age is only interested in a science about bad ones."[456] For Chesterton, as for many people from Voltaire onward, the contrast between the Dark Ages — an ironic reference to the medieval period — and the modern Enlightenment has to do

Quixote (1927) contains a full and amusing satire on the sentimental preoccupation with the externals of medieval life which neglects those essential values which alone gave it meaning" (J. D. Coates, *Chesterton as Controversialist, Essayist, Novelist, and Critic*, 184).

[455]*Chaucer: A Study*, 293.

[456]*The Complete Father Brown Stories*, 516.

with the hegemony or the marginalisation, respectively, of the Catholic Church, though Chesterton's evaluation of that contrast was rather different from Voltaire's. How Chesterton saw the Church, first as an Anglo-Catholic, then as [Roman] Catholic, must be our next topic.

Chapter 9

Chesterton and the Church

Chesterton was, of course, concerned with the Church long before he entered peace and communion with the See of Rome. In his Anglo-Catholic period his Churchmanship was, however, not terribly engaged, except in controversy. Surprisingly, he seems to have participated very little in the rich liturgical life of the Anglo-Catholic parishes to which his wife's faithfulness of practice and his own reputation as an Anglo-Catholic Sir Galahad would surely have given him ready access. This should not prevent us from taking seriously the ecclesiological elements in his earlier works, and above all in *Orthodoxy*'s sixth chapter, "The Paradoxes of Christianity," which, while it hardly touches on the structure of the Church — as organic community, hierarchical society, or whatever — has plenty to say about the Church's moral, ascetical, devotional, and credal life.

Ecclesial Paradox in Orthodoxy

In *Orthodoxy* Chesterton recounts how struck he was by the contrariety of the objections brought against the Church for being both deplorably X and lamentably non-X at one and the same time. This is where the application of paradox to ecclesiology, flagged by

G. K. Chesterton, Theologian

Denis, comes into its own. If, pondered Chesterton, re-creating the mindset of his still uncommitted days:

> this mass of mad contradictions really existed, quakerish and blood-thirsty, too gorgeous and too thread-bare, austere, yet pandering preposterously to the lust of the eye, the enemy of women and their foolish refuge, a solemn pessimist and a silly optimist, if this evil existed, then there was in this evil something quite supreme and unique . . . Such a paradox of evil rose to the stature of the Supernatural . . . An historic institution, which never went right, is really quite as much of a miracle as an institution that cannot go wrong.[457]

Chesterton's first reaction was: Perhaps Christ — and therefore the Church of Christ — is the Antichrist. His second reaction was, if a man is criticised for being the wrong shape by critics who flatly contradict each other in their attempts to say just what is wrong about him, quite possibly he is quite the right shape after all. In Chesterton's example:

> [I]t was certainly odd that the modern world charged Christianity at once with bodily austerity and with artistic pomp. But then it was also odd, very odd, that the modern world itself combined extreme bodily luxury with an extreme absence of artistic pomp. The modern man thought Becket's robes too rich and his meals too poor. But then the modern man was really exceptional in history; no man before ever ate such elaborate dinners in such ugly clothes.[458]

---

[457]*Orthodoxy*, 129.
[458]Ibid., 130-131.

Thinking constructively on the point, Chesterton divined that the Church had maintained the Aristotelean insight that virtue lies in a mean, a middle way, in Greek *meson*. But she had understood this in an altogether distinctive fashion. She had understood it to mean a "moderation made from the still crash of two impetuous emotions."[459] The key lies, he thought, in the overall gospel message about Creation, Fall, and Redemption, which furnishes us with two contrasting, yet not for that reason mutually exclusive, truths. Chesterton writes:

> In one way Man was to be haughtier than he had ever been before; in another way he was to be humbler than he had ever been before. Insofar as I am Man, I am the chief of creatures. Insofar as I am a man, I am the chief of sinners . . . Christianity thus held a thought of the dignity of man that could only be expressed in crowns rayed like the sun and fans of peacock plumage. Yet at the same time it could hold a thought about the abject smallness of man that could only be expressed in fasting and fantastic submission, in the gray ashes of St Dominic and the white snows of St Bernard.[460]

Francis of Assisi in his praise of good could be a more blatant optimist than Whitman; Jerome of Bethlehem, in his denunciation of evil, could be a blacker pessimist than Schopenhauer. And the explanation is that "both passions were free because both were kept in their place."[461]

The "historic church" has emphasised both celibacy and the family. It has told some men to fight and others not to fight. It has

[459]Ibid., 135.
[460]Ibid., 136-137.
[461]Ibid., 139.

sanctioned both asceticism and celebration — and each in relation to the other.

> Because a man prayed and fasted on the Northern snows,
> flowers could be flung at his festival in the Southern cities;
> and because fanatics drank water on the sands of Syria, men
> could still drink cider in the orchards of England.[462]

Care in the Formulation of Doctrine

"Mental and emotional liberty," observed Chesterton, "are not so simple as they look."[463] The Church "had to be careful," not least so that the "world might be careless."[464] Hence the great care that had to be invested in the formulation of doctrine. The Church "went in specifically for dangerous ideas; she was a lion-tamer."[465]

> The idea of birth through a Holy Spirit, of the death of a
> divine being, of the forgiveness of sins, or the fulfilment of
> prophecies, are ideas which, anyone can see, need but a
> touch to turn them into something blasphemous or fero-
> cious. The smallest link was let drop by the artificers of the
> Mediterranean, and the lion of ancestral pessimism burst
> his chain in the forgotten forests of the North.[466]

The Church taught Chesterton that the "thrilling romance of Orthodoxy" is also a remarkable sanity. But as he adds, "to be sane is more dramatic than to be mad": it is the "equilibrium of a man

---

[462] *Orthodoxy*, 144.
[463] Ibid., 138.
[464] Ibid., 146.
[465] Ibid., 145.
[466] Ibid.

behind madly rushing horses."[467] And it was in that spirit that he "accepted Christendom" as his "mother."[468] A "living teacher," it (or she) "not only certainly taught me yesterday, but will almost certainly teach me tomorrow."[469] Evidently, he expected further truths from the treasury of the deposit of faith to strike home before he died.

The Atmosphere of a Fresh Conversion

What Chesterton did not know in 1908, though the play he makes between the words "romance" and "Rome" perhaps indicates some surmise, was that Christendom would teach him the wider circle of truths into which he entered in 1922 with his move from the Church of England to the Catholic Church. One cannot imagine Chesterton at any time of his life glued to church newspapers or perusing pastoral letters. Like Evelyn Waugh, he probably regarded a detailed interest in ecclesiastical affairs on the part of laymen as a telltale sign of incipient lunacy. As he put it, more gently, in *The Catholic Church and Conversion*: "[I]n most communions the ecclesiastical layman is more ecclesiastical than is good for his health, and certainly much more ecclesiastical than the ecclesiastics."[470] Even so, it is not surprising that his conversion to Catholicism triggered a new phase of writing of a more focussed ecclesiological kind. This was a momentous shift of allegiance to a form of Christianity which, in England, had been, ever since the seventeenth century, deeply unpopular or, at any rate, suspect. After the failure of the second Jacobite uprising in

[467] Ibid., 146.
[468] Ibid., 232.
[469] Ibid., 230.
[470] *The Catholic Church and Conversion* (London, 1926), 40.

1745, the spread of Enlightenment tolerance combined with the discretion of the recusant minority to improve matters. But the situation was soon re-inflamed with the nineteenth-century mass immigration of Irish paupers and the fears of crypto-Romanism in the Church of England that the Tractarian and Ritualist movements enkindled. Dislike of Catholicism has been called, no doubt too cynically, the default religion of the English. Its last dramatic public manifestation (so far) was in the year when Chesterton published *Orthodoxy*, 1908. An international Eucharistic Congress was held in London. The Metropolitan Police announced they would be unable to guarantee public order if the monstrance containing the eucharistic host were carried through the streets of the capital.

Would such ill will have worried Chesterton? *Did* it worry him? Did he, as some think, fear a diminution of Englishness? Well, the problem was scarcely confined to England. He noted later "the sincere and savage hatred felt by many Europeans for the religion of their own European past."[471] And in any case, like John Henry Newman when writing the *Essay on the Development of Christian Doctrine*, he was inclined to think that the penchant of the Catholic Church for attracting hostility was a sign of its identity with the Church of early Christian times. The story of the Church is, he thought:

> the story of . . . something which is always coming out of the Catacombs and going back again, something that is never entirely acceptable when it appears, and never entirely forgotten when it disappears.[472]

---

[471] *The Glass Walking-stick, and Other Essays*, 60.
[472] Ibid., p. 63.

His Apologia

Chesterton's principal apologia was, as its title suggests, his 1926 *The Catholic Church and Conversion*.[473] Among other things, *The Catholic Church and Conversion* sought to deconstruct the English, British, or Anglo-Saxon tradition of popular anti-Catholicism: a necessary step if Chesterton were to capture the good will of his readership.[474] That tradition had certain recurrent features, from the lasciviousness of nuns to the shiftiness of Jesuits. Newman, who had much the same aims as Chesterton in his *Lectures on the Present Position of Catholics in England*, parodies anti-Catholicism with almost Dickensian *grotesquerie*,[475] whereas Chesterton shows a lighter touch. For example, on the topic of Jesuit equivocation, Chesterton considers it absurd to

> pillory half a dozen Popish priests for a crime committed daily by half a million Protestant laymen . . . Every gentleman was expected to say he would be delighted to dine with a bore; every lady said that somebody else's baby was beautiful if she thought it as ugly as sin . . .[476]

If Chesterton's apologia seems at times a little half-hearted, that may be because, as he admits, he personally had never felt the force of the anti-Catholic tradition, owing to the liberal atmosphere created by his parents. While showing no sympathy with

---

[473]Two of Chesterton's essay collections also throw further light on his thinking: *The Thing*, published in 1929, and *The Well and The Shallows*, published in 1935, the year before his death.

[474]See P. Jenkins, "Chesterton and the Anti-Catholic Tradition," *The Chesterton Review* XVIII, 3 (1992): 345-370.

[475]I. Ker, *The Catholic Revival in English Literature (1845-1961): Newman, Hopkins, Belloc, Chesterton, Greene, Waugh* (Notre Dame, Indiana, 2003), 22.

[476]*The Catholic Church and Conversion*, 22.

Catholics, they wanted nevertheless to be just to them. "I was always sufficiently enlightened to be out of the reach of Maria Monk,"[477] a reference to the Victorian penny dreadful which summed up the popular "black legend."

The only aspect of anti-Popery he really bothers to take seriously is the claim that a Catholic cannot be a patriot. For Catholicism, he argues, patriotism is simply one aspect of being human: "we must love all men; but what do all men love? They love their lands, their lawful boundaries, the memories of their fathers."[478] Patriotism is not a superordinate consideration that trumps all others, whereas when the Englishman beats the Protestant drum, it often seems to be just that. The trouble is that "the normal British subject begins by being so very British."[479] The Catholic Church, on the other hand, began in "a vast cosmopolitan cosmos that had never heard the name of England," namely, the Roman empire.[480] So that Church can only "love nations as she loves men; because they are her children."[481]

There are also arguments, as distinct from prejudices, which inhibit access to Catholicism. In many cases, these arguments by their diametrical opposition to each other tend to cancel each other out, since, for example, the universalist curses Rome for "having too much predestination," the Calvinist curses her for "having too little"; one "No Popery man" finds her doctrine of Purgatory "too

---

[477] *The Catholic Church and Conversion*, 16.

[478] Ibid., 29.

[479] Ibid., 30. In his *Autobiography* he suggested that imperialism, or, at any rate, patriotism, had become a substitute religion for many British people. "Men believed in the British Empire precisely because they had no thing else to believe in" (145).

[480] *The Catholic Church and Conversion*, 30.

[481] Ibid., 31.

tender-hearted," another finds her doctrine of Hell "too harsh."[482] This state of affairs is exactly analogous to the situation Chesterton found to be the case with objections to "Christendom" in *Orthodoxy*, where he concluded that someone found so inconsistently to be always wrong might actually be right.

What holds more people back is, he thinks, the sense of moral demand found in a Church that uses auricular confession in its administration of Penance, and, more widely, wields pastoral authority in the service of a clear moral code. The expectation of realistic sincerity in the confessional frightens people. And the reason is that "most modern realists only like [realism] because they are careful to be realistic about other people."[483] And more widely the convert will have to be more responsible:

> He will have somebody to be responsible to and he will know what he is responsible for; two uncomfortable conditions which his more fortunate fellow creatures have nowadays entirely escaped.[484]

Once these obstacles are overcome — if they *are* overcome — the person is free to discover the Church, a process Chesterton describes as easier than joining it and much easier than trying to live its life. He compares the discovery to finding "a new continent full of strange flowers and fantastic animals, which is at once wild and hospitable."[485]

There now intervenes, so Chesterton claims in what we can call his phenomenology of the conversion process, an "interval of

---

[482] Ibid., 36.
[483] Ibid., 38.
[484] Ibid., 39.
[485] Ibid., 45.

intense nervousness" before someone takes the plunge, rather as with the shaky bridegroom at the wedding or the army recruit who takes the king's shilling and gets drunk partly to celebrate but partly to forget. Its content is anxiety that what previously seemed so bad as to be intolerable now seems too good to be true. But if nonetheless someone actually joins the Catholic Church, Chesterton predicts the chief effect will be one of stepping into a larger room.

> At the last moment of all, the convert often feels as if he were looking through a leper's window. He is looking through a little crack or crooked hole that seems to grow smaller as he stares at it; but it is an opening that looks towards the Altar. Only, when he has entered the Church, he finds that the Church is much larger inside than it is outside. He has left behind him the lop-sidedness of lepers' windows and even in a sense the narrowness of Gothic doors; and he is under vast domes as open as the Renaissance and as universal as the Republic of the world.[486]

Entering a Wider Realm

The experience of entering this wider space is discussed by Chesterton under the heading "The world inside out." The basic idea here is that revelation as transmitted in the Catholic Church is the greatest possible truth that can be conceived. All other truths, whatever their provenance, can fit into this truth but it cannot fit into them. In *The Thing*, Chesterton applies this to Calvinists who "took the Catholic idea of the absolute knowledge and power of God," and to Evangelicals who "seized on the very

---

[486]*The Catholic Church and Conversion*, 49.

Catholic idea that mankind has a sense of sin,"[487] but also to those outside Christianity in any form, such as the atheistic poets Shelley and Whitman and the "revolutionary optimists" (presumably, from the Great Revolution of the West, 1789-1815) who had "taken out of the old Catholic tradition one particular transcendental idea; the idea that there is a spiritual dignity in man as man, and a universal duty to love men as men."[488] That was the nugget of gold which Chesterton, following Belloc's example, took from the French revolutionaries' "Declaration of the Rights of Man and of the Citizen." Many elements of Catholic truth, then, are found outside Catholicism altogether. As Chesterton puts it in *The Catholic Church and Conversion*:

> [The convert] is not worried by being told that there is something in Spiritualism or something in Christian Science. He knows there is something in everything. But he is moved by the more impressive fact that he finds everything in something.[489]

If that is somewhat oracular, Chesterton spells it out when he writes:

> The outsiders stand by and see, or think they see, the convert entering with bowed head a sort of small temple which they are convinced is fitted up inside like a prison, if not a torture-chamber. But all they really know about it is that he has passed through a door. They do not know that he has not gone into the inner darkness, but out into the broad daylight. It is he who is, in the broad and beautiful sense of

[487] *The Thing*, 29.
[488] Ibid., 30.
[489] *The Catholic Church and Conversion*, 67.

the word, an outsider. He does not want to go into a larger room, because he does not know of any larger room to go into. He knows of a large number of much smaller rooms, each of which is labelled as being very large; but he is quite sure he would be cramped in any of them. Each of them professes to be a complete cosmos or scheme of all things . . . Each of them is supposed to be domed with the sky or painted inside with all the stars. But each of these cosmic systems or machines seems to him much smaller and even much simpler than the broad and balanced universe in which he lives.[490]

That is, clearly, the Chesterton of *Orthodoxy* speaking and it justifies, up to a point, the claim of the Canadian Chesterton scholar Ian Boyd that Chesterton's conversion "was the result of a personal decision that had more to do with a question of fact than a change in his religious convictions."[491]

But what fact? Chesterton tells us himself in *The Catholic Church and Conversion* when he writes:

There are High Churchmen as much as Low Churchmen who are concerned first and last to save the Church of England. Some of them think it can be saved by calling it Catholic, or making it Catholic, or believing that it is Catholic; but *that* is what they want to save. But I did not start out with the idea of saving the English Church, but of finding the Catholic Church. If the two were one, so much the better; but I had never conceived of Catholicism as a sort of showy attribute or attraction to be tacked on to my

[490]*The Catholic Church and Conversion*, 68.

[491]I. Boyd, *The Novels of G. K. Chesterton*, xii.

own national body, but as the inmost soul of the true body, wherever it might be. It might be said [concluded Chesterton] that Anglo-Catholicism was simply my own uncompleted conversion to Catholicism.[492]

A Last Look Back

That was in 1926, though. How did things look ten years later at the end of his life? The best guide is *The Well and the Shallows* published the year before he died. Chesterton looks back on the intervening decade to discuss what he calls his "post-conversion conversion," by which he means, as he explains, things that have happened since his reception into the Church of Rome, things which "would in any case have rendered impossible any intellectual position outside the Church, and especially the position in which I originally found myself."[493] The six trends or episodes he names under this rubric are very various. But at least they show what Chesterton considered momentous, what was preoccupying him most, in the last years of his life.

The first is the fossilisation of Protestantism as evidenced by the growth of Anglican Modernism on the one hand and, across the North Sea, the emergence of the Nazi-sponsored so-called "German Christianity" on the other. "Fossilisation" seems an odd term for vigorous if misguided religious movements, but Chesterton explains its use here well enough when he writes:

A fossil is not a dead animal, or a decayed organism, or in essence even an antiquated object. The whole point of a fossil is that it is the *form* of an animal or organism, from

[492] Ibid., 19.
[493] *The Well and the Shallows*, 23.

which all its own animal or organic substance has entirely disappeared; but which has kept its shape, because it has been filled up by some totally different substance by some process of distillation or secretion, so that we might almost say, as in the mediaeval metaphysics, that its substance has vanished and only its accidents remain.[494]

The substance of Christianity is evaporating, Chesterton was claiming, from the historic churches of the Reformation.

His second reflection on "post-conversion conversion" concerned the rise of the Fascist dictators, a political seismic shift which reversed the Victorian consensus about the "way the world was going" — towards, that is, greater freedom and fraternity in a context of representative democracy. The lesson of the "age of the dictators" for Chesterton was:

put not your trust in manhood suffrage or in any child of man. There is one little defect about Man, the image of God, the wonder of the world and the paragon of animals; that he is not to be trusted. If you identify him with some ideal, which you choose to think is his inmost nature or his only goal, the day will come when he will suddenly seem to you a traitor.[495]

That might not seem to have any particular relevance to Catholicism as such, but the moral Chesterton draws from it is in keeping with his earlier claims that humanism may be the pool, but Christendom is the fountain — namely, modernity is exhausting Catholic capital. He writes, and it is no more than a free assertion which may therefore be as freely denied:

[494]*The Well and the Shallows*, 25.
[495]Ibid., 34.

[I]n the centre of the civilisation called Catholic, there and in no movement and in no future, is found that crystallisation of commonsense and true traditions and rational reforms, for which the modern man mistakenly looked to the trend of the modern age.[496]

Chesterton's third crisis concerns what he calls "the surrender upon sex," his name for two worrying developments: the decision of the 1930 Lambeth Conference to accept the use of artificial birth control within marriage, and a series of indications that Anglicans were preparing to accept likewise the Church remarriage of the divorced. "Modern Churchmen" argued for this departure from traditional Christian sexual discipline as progressive. This was not a way to Chesterton's heart. Continuous change, he conceded, could be called progress, just as "a snow-man, slowly turning into a puddle" could be said to be "purifying itself of its accretions."[497] In sexual matters, whether in external codes or in "deeper matters," the "modern will," he thought, has been amazingly "weak and wavering."[498] It was proposed to allow birth-prevention or divorce in special circumstances. Chesterton countered: "The Catholic Church, standing almost alone, declared that [this] would in fact lead to an anarchical position; and the Catholic Church was right."[499]

Chesterton's fourth converting issue was the controversy in the Church of England over the 1928 revision of the Prayer Book, which Parliament notoriously rejected against the wishes of the Church Assembly and the Anglican bishops of the day. The members of the House of Commons, wrote Chesterton:

[496]Ibid., 35.
[497]Ibid., 38.
[498]Ibid., 40.
[499]Ibid., 42.

whether they claimed to be Protestants or clamorously bragged of being atheists . . . all seemed to have this fixed idea; that they owned the Church of England; and could turn it into a Mormon temple if they liked.[500]

And he adds, "I could not, in any case, have gone on being owned in that way."[501]

The fifth issue in his catalogue was very different, and hardly seems to have much in the way of obvious implications for the Anglican/Catholic distinction. Chesterton entitled it "collapse of materialism." In his interpretation of the theoretical physics of the 1920s and '30s, such figures as, in Germany, Albert Einstein or, in Britain, Sir Arthur Eddington, were saying that science no longer had any conclusive answers to the question "What ultimately is real?" The only specifically Catholic "take" Chesterton can offer on this is that the Church "throws down the unanswered challenge of Lourdes,"[502] a reference to the investigations of inexplicable cures by the Medical Bureau at that town of the 1858 Marian apparitions, though he also mentions that the "youngest school of Catholic apologists," with figures like Ronald Knox, Arnold Lunn, and Christopher Hollis, were, in his opinion, bringing a new rigour to bear on their arguments about such Gospel miracles as the Resurrection of Christ.[503]

Chesterton's last "post-conversion conversion" moment he calls "the case of Spain." The Spanish Civil War broke out just as Chesterton died, but the conflagration was, of course, already brewing. After his death, the Distributists — and indeed other

[500] Ibid., 45.
[501] Ibid.
[502] Ibid., 55.
[503] Ibid., 56.

Chestertonians — disagreed violently over what might have been his reaction to the War had he lived. Chesterton had no quarrel with the declaration of a Republic in Spain, but he most definitely quarrelled with the support English Liberals gave to Spanish Socialists who in his view threatened the forcible disruption of civil government unless the Cortes accepted a radical anti-clericalism which had failed to triumph in the popular vote. The rallying of English Liberalism to Socialist anti-clericalism in Spain completed the political disillusion begun by his observation of financial corruption in the Liberal government before the First World War. And his conclusion, which we might think somewhat premature, was:

> [T]here are no Fascists; there are no Socialists; there are no Liberals; there are no Parliamentarians. There is the one supremely inspiring and irritating institution in the world; and there are its enemies.[504]

These six affairs or tendencies aside, we could sum up the temper of Chesterton's Catholicism in his last year with the words that allude to the title of the book from which these extracts are taken: "We have come out of the shallows and the dry places to the one deep well; and the Truth is at the bottom of it."[505] Looking back, doubtless on his own career as well as that of others, Chesterton noted:

> We have done far less than we should have done, to explain all that balance of subtlety and sanity which is meant by a Christian civilisation . . . We did not ourselves think that

[504]Ibid., 64.
[505]*The Well and the Shallows*, 72.

the mere denial of our dogmas could end in such dehumanised and demented anarchy . . . We did not believe that rationalists were so utterly mad until they made it quite clear to us . . . We have done very little against them; *non nobis, Domine*; the glory of their final overthrow is all their own.[506]

In the struggle against what he called the "recent riot and vulgarity of the merely 'modern' world,"[507] Chesterton would have liked to say that his mature adulthood had witnessed a "popular revolt" of "ordinary, old-fashioned, obstinate people" against the "perversions and pedantries of vice."[508] In this wish, we can see how his populism endured to the end. But he had been, he had to confess, not only disappointed but surprised. There *was* a revolt, but it was led by T. S. Eliot and Aldous Huxley.

God moves in a mysterious way [concluded Chesterton] and does not disdain the strangest or the humblest instruments; and we must not be ashamed of finding ourselves, if necessary, on the side of the cultivated and the clever.[509]

---

[506]*The Well and the Shallows*, 79.
[507]Ibid., 91.
[508]Ibid., 92.
[509]Ibid., 92-03.

Conclusion

It seems an appropriately Chestertonian pun that an inventory of his theological contribution should end with eschatology, thus concluding with the Conclusion of the world. The ending of his study of Dickens provides us with an entrée. Chesterton is asking after the ultimate direction toward which Dickens's characteristically *English* achievement points. What the dickens did Dickens mean? Chesterton's answer introduces the topic of the character of eternity, understood as the life of man in God. He responds:

> [T]his at least is part of what he meant; that comradeship and serious joy are not interludes in our travel; but that rather our travels are interludes in comradeship and joy, which through God shall endure for ever. The inn [the reference must be to *The Pickwick Papers*] does not point to the road; the road points to the inn.[510]

And Chesterton draws a wider conclusion which forms his own version of the classical eschatological themes of the Communion of Saints and the messianic banquet: "And all roads point at

---

[510]*Charles Dickens*, 297.

last to an ultimate inn, where we shall meet Dickens and all his characters: and when we drink again it shall be from the great flagons in the tavern at the end of the world."[511] This is a passage which some have flagged as an example of Chesterton's hearty, Merrie-England-ish, pseudo-mediaeval jollity, though as a matter of fact it raises a question not much addressed, so far as I am aware, by theologians: namely, what is the status of characters from fiction — sub-created literary beings — in the divine mind?

In the context of Chesterton's work, these citations from *Charles Dickens* suggest, if not an answer to the theological question I just raised, then at least a response to the literary question Chesterton himself raised when writing another of his scintillating studies of the novelists, *Robert Louis Stevenson*. "There is," wrote Chesterton in that work:

> at the back of every artist's mind something like a pattern or a type of architecture. The original quality in any man of imagination is imagery. It is a thing like the landscapes of his dreams; the sort of world he would wish to make or in which he would wish to wander; the strange flora and fauna of his own secret planet; the *sort* of thing he likes to think about. This general atmosphere, and pattern or structure of growth, governs all his creations, however varied, and because he can in this sense create a world, he is in this sense a creator; the image of God.[512]

In Chesterton's case — this, at least, is my proposal — the "pattern" in question could be described as a wonderful adventure of discovery, ending in the greatest discovery of all, coming home,

---

[511]*Charles Dickens*, 297.

[512]*Robert Louis Stevenson*, 40.

coming to the *Patria*. An inn is not quite a home, though inns were, I suppose, homes from home for Chesterton. Still, the parallel with the ending of *Charles Dickens* is near enough.

In any case, the point of a pattern or a "type of architecture" in literary creation is its formation, as Chesterton writes, of an overall atmosphere or ethos. It does not have to be adverted to very often in order to be felt. The consummation of all things in the Age to Come when the world goes home is not as such a frequently invoked motif in Chesterton. But it *is* signalled explicitly from time to time. In *The Ball and the Cross* MacIan is found explaining how "an apocalypse is the opposite of a dream": "A dream is falser than the outer life. But the end of the world is more actual than the world it ends . . . Everything is coming to a point."[513]

Chesterton's aim of reviving the romance of Christianity, and its confident hope for homecoming in God, by a wide re-diffusion of its ethos — what he termed "Christendom" — was not realised in the second half of the twentieth century in either Britain in particular or Western Europe in general. Rather. the opposite was the case. But as one social historian has observed: "The most decisive secularization may cause dissatisfactions that prepare the way for ultimate revival."[514] That thought is a cause for hope, even if it also implies that tears will be shed on the way. Chesterton's regret for his own contemporaries, in an era dominated by scientism and the Nietzschean will to power, was that those who sought to preserve human values held to them less firmly than might have been the case had they possessed an appropriate metaphysic, and a

[513]*The Ball and the Cross*, 377.

[514]H. McLeod, "Secular Cities? Berlin, London, and New York in the Later Nineteenth and Early Twentieth Centuries," in S. Bruce, ed., *Religion and Modernization: Sociologists and Historians Debate the Secularization Thesis* (Oxford, 1992), 86.

groundwork of morals to match. Writing shortly after Chesterton's death, T. S. Eliot testified that, even if his ideas appeared to be totally without effect, "they were the ideas for his time that were fundamentally Christian and Catholic. He did more, I think, than any man of his time . . . to maintain the existence of the important minority in the modern world."[515]

After all, the final *dénouement* which, by the faith of the Church, he expected to be marvellous, was also not to be attained without human struggle or divine drama: "When evil things become evil, good things, in a blazing apocalypse, become good."[516]

---

[515]Cited in D. J. Conlon, ed., G. K. Chesterton: The Critical Judgments (Antwerp, 1976), 531-532.

[516]*Charles Dickens*, 284.

Bibliography

Primary Bibliography

The project of publishing in a uniform series the *Collected Works of G. K. Chesterton* was begun by Ignatius Press of San Francisco in 1986. A listing of individual works and contributions, according to their original place and date of publication is found in:

Sullivan, J. *G. K. Chesterton: A Bibliography, with an Essay on Books by G. K. Chesterton and an Epitaph by Walter de la Mare.* London, 1958.

——. *Chesterton Continued: A Bibliographical Supplement.* London, 1968.

The reader keen to do research will find useful:

Sprug, J. W. (ed.). *An Index to G. K. Chesterton.* Washington, 1966.

Secondary Bibliography

Barker, D. *G. K. Chesterton: A Biography.* London, 1958.

Boyd, I., [C.S.B.]. *The Novels of G. K. Chesterton.* London, 1975.

G. K. Chesterton, Theologian

Canovan, M. G. K. Chesterton: Radical Populist (New York, 1977).

Coates, J. D. Chesterton and the Edwardian Cultural Crisis. Hull, 1984.

————. G. K. Chesterton as Controversialist, Essayist, Novelist, and Critic. Lewiston, NY, 2002.

Clipper, L. J. G. K. Chesterton. New York, 1974.

Conlon, D. J., ed. G. K. Chesterton: The Critical Judgments. Antwerp, 1976.

————, ed. G. K. Chesterton: A Half Century of Views. Oxford, 1987.

Coren, M. Gilbert: The Man who was G. K. Chesterton. London, 1989.

Crowther, I. G. K.Chesterton. London, 1991.

Dale, A. S. The Outline of Sanity: A Biography of G. K. Chesterton. Grand Rapids, Michigan, 1982.

Denis, Y. G. K. Chesterton: Paradoxe et Catholicisme. Paris, 1978.

Jaki, S. L. Chesterton, a Seer of Science. Urbana, Illinois, and Chicago, 1986.

Ker, I. The Catholic Revival in English Literature (1845-1961): Newman, Hopkins, Belloc, Chesterton, Greene, Waugh. Notre Dame, Indiana, 2003.

Kenner, H. Paradox in Chesterton. London, 1948.

Milbank, A. Chesterton and Tolkien as Theologians: The Fantasy of the Real. London, 2007.

Nichols, A., O.P., ed. *Chesterton and the Modernist Crisis*. Saskatoon, 1990.

Oddie, W. *Chesterton and the Romance of Orthodoxy. The Making of GKC 1874-1908*. Oxford, 2008.

Pearce, J. *Wisdom and Innocence: A Life of G. K. Chesterton*. San Francisco, 1997.

Reckitt, M. *G. K. Chesterton: A Christian Prophet for England Today*. London, 1950.

Schwartz, A. *The Third Spring: G. K. Chesterton, Graham Greene, Christopher Dawson, and David Jones*. Washington 2005.

Sullivan, J., ed. *G. K. Chesterton: A Centenary Appraisal*. New York, 1974.

Ward, M. *Gilbert Keith Chesterton*. London, 1944.

————. *Return to Chesterton*. London, 1952.

Wills, G. *Chesterton: Man and Mask*. New York, 1961.

Aidan Nichols, O.P.

Fr. Aidan Nichols, O.P., of Blackfriars, Cambridge, is a member of the Divinity Faculty of Cambridge University and possibly the most prolific writer of theology in the English language. He has published on countless topics, especially in systematic, sacramental, and ecumenical theology, and was awarded the title *Sacrae Theologiae Magister* by the Dominican order in 2003. His books include important studies of St Thomas Aquinas; modern thinkers, including Hans Urs von Balthasar; and the theology of Pope Benedict XVI. He has written on the liturgical "reform of the reform" and on "re-energising the Church in Culture," as well as on the arts and iconography. The present book is based on a series of lectures given as the John Paul II Memorial Lecturer at the University of Oxford — the first Catholic Lectureship created in the university since the Reformation.

Second Spring
from
SOPHIA INSTITUTE PRESS

To all who work for the reintegration of faith and reason in the Liberal Arts, *Second Spring* books offer help, guidance, and inspiration, fostering in those who read them a love of learning and the desire for God.

Published as a joint venture of *Second Spring: A Journal of Faith and Culture*, Thomas More College, and Sophia Institute Press®, *Second Spring* books are scholarly, but accessible to non-scholars who yearn to be formed by the ideas and values found in the Catholic tradition of humane letters.

Sophia Institute Press®

Sophia Institute® is a nonprofit institution that seeks to restore man's knowledge of eternal truth, including man's knowledge of his own nature, his relation to other persons, and his relation to God. Sophia Institute Press® serves this end in numerous ways: it publishes translations of foreign works to make them accessible for the first time to English-speaking readers; it brings out-of-print books back into print; and it publishes important new books that fulfill the ideals of Sophia Institute®. These books afford readers a rich source of the enduring wisdom of mankind.

For your free catalog, call:
Toll-free: 1-800-888-9344
or write:
Sophia Institute Press®
Box 5284, Manchester, NH 03108
or visit our website:
www.SophiaInstitute.com

Sophia Institute® is a tax-exempt institution as defined by the Internal Revenue Code, Section 501(c)(3). Tax I.D. 22-2548708.

CPSIA information can be obtained at www.ICGtesting.com
Printed in the USA
BVOW08s1652030214

343654BV00001B/2/P